Hope you enjoy TGAL!
-
Bo Brink

THE GREATEST ANIMAL LOVER

Our Special Bond with Them Originates in Him

BO BRINK

WESTBOW
PRESS®
A DIVISION OF THOMAS NELSON
& ZONDERVAN

WestBow Press books may be ordered through booksellers or by contacting:

WestBow Press
A Division of Thomas Nelson & Zondervan
1663 Liberty Drive
Bloomington, IN 47403
www.westbowpress.com
1 (866) 928-1240

Scriptures taken from the Holy Bible, New International Version®,
NIV®. Copyright © 1973, 1978, 1984, 2011 by Biblica, Inc.™ Used by
permission of Zondervan. All rights reserved worldwide. www.zondervan.
com The "NIV" and "New International Version" are trademarks registered
in the United States Patent and Trademark Office by Biblica, Inc.™

ISBN: 978-1-9736-7827-4 (sc)
ISBN: 978-1-9736-7829-8 (hc)
ISBN: 978-1-9736-7828-1 (e)

Library of Congress Control Number: 2019916975

Print information available on the last page.

WestBow Press rev. date: 11/08/2019

Thanks to Barb, Toby, Marion, Karla Kay and Hannah
for making *The Greatest Animal Lover* readable!

CONTENTS

INTRODUCTION

Humans Love and Admire Animals

Wow! We humans think the world of animals! Wouldn't you agree this truth is on display all around us?

A friend of mine and I were visiting at a coffee shop here in Las Vegas. It was a typical, beautiful Vegas January day. A man was sitting outside in the sun, sipping at his coffee, and attempting to read a book. Resting beside him was his golden retriever. The dog was large, with thick brown hair and eyes which said to everyone who walked by, "Hey, I think I like you a lot. I'd love to have you pet me and be my friend." My buddy and I were there for about 30 minutes. Of 20 people who walked by the dog, about 18 couldn't resist his invitation. They stopped to admire, pet, and speak kind words to the dog, and of course, to his owner. I've never seen anyone get so little reading done in a half hour. He should have left his book in the car and put a little sign on his table which read, "Yes, it's OK; let's talk about my dog."

At the same time, about 20 feet away were a man and two ladies trying to have an informal business meeting. Their problem was that the man had brought his T-Rex-sized, black Great Dane. The dog was calm, friendly, and affectionate. He was sitting behind his owner and several times lifted his front paws and put them over his master's shoulders to give him a hug, resting his huge head on his owner's head. Those of us inside the coffee shop gasped each time the dog did this. Almost everyone who passed by gawked at the dog and interrupted the meeting asking the same question: "May I pet your dog?" Their first touch was always rather hesitant, knowing that if for some reason the dog didn't like them, they were dead meat. But he liked them all and didn't want them to stop! Very little business was achieved but much animal admiration took place.

My neighbor Roy has a bird, a young conure parrot. She is beautiful from beak to butt feathers. Sometimes she is in a good mood and warmhearted, and other times she is cranky and enjoys pooping on and biting her owner. Yet Roy loves this bird and she loves Roy. The bird sits on Roy's shoulder and they talk and joke and laugh. As time goes by, their bond grows deeper!

When I was a little boy, we had a beautiful calico cat named Pregnant Pam. When she was nine years old, she was walking across the backyard and keeled over dead. I imagine this was because in her first eight years she had 64 kittens! But Pam was part of our family, and I loved her and her many kittens. As a young lad, I needed two things to be able to fall asleep: a backrub from Grandpa, and the purring of Pam next to my head on the pillow. This was almost 60 years ago, yet I still have great memories of that cat! How about you? Do you have fond memories of a childhood pet?

My friends Nick and Barb had a golden retriever named Buck. For years this dog brought joy, love, and laughter to their home. Buck has been gone for eight years but is not forgotten. Today Buck's ashes are on the hearth in their living room and Nick and Barb still think about Buck every day.

My brother-in-law, Rick, has a deep love for cats. It shows in his reflections on the death of his beloved cat, Cleo.

So, my dear little Cleo,
Thank you for nearly fourteen years of sweet companionship.
Thank you for the silly toys, the silly games, the silly nips and swats, and all the many ways you made me laugh.

Thank you for the beauty of the quiet, meditative
purring moments that highlighted our early mornings.
Thank you for running to the door to greet me every
evening when I would return from the day away.
Thank you for being you and being with me. Your
presence has been one of my life's richest blessings.
Thank you, dear Cleo. You are always in my heart.

Have you ever felt this way about a pet?

To many humans, horses are man's best friend. My good friend Dave is from Montana and had a mare named Nicky for 28 years. They would go exploring and camping together in the Bob Marshall Wilderness. They were best friends, so when Nicky died, it took Dave a long time to get over her passing. Have you had a horse which was your best friend?

While writing this book, I saw an internet video of a beautiful tiger which was loose in a city in India. He looked so scared. He tackled a few people, but didn't hurt them seriously, though he could have killed them instantaneously. The people were very frightened, but nobody wanted the tiger dead. Surely someone could have shot and killed it, but no one did. It took authorities an hour and a half to get a tranquilizer dart into the tiger, which was then carefully carried away to an appropriate animal shelter. All over the world, humans show care and concern for both tame and wild animals.

Animals Are Abundant in Our Media

Our TV shows are full of animals. If you're an oldie like me, you probably affectionately remember the animal TV shows of the 50's and 60's, such as *Mr. Ed, Lassie, Flipper, Benji, and Rin-Tin-Tin.* We can't think of Roy Rogers without Trigger or the Lone Ranger without Silver. And our younger generations are growing up watching *Nature Cat, Curious George, Paw Patrol,* and many more! We also love to watch movies about animals. Our hearts have been touched by *Homeward Bound, Ice Age, Old Yeller, Marley and Me, War Horse, Dog's Purpose, Hachi: A Dog's Tale, Dr. Doolittle, and Madagascar.* Do you remember *Babe, Charlotte's Web, 101 Dalmatians,* or *Free Willy?* How about *Two Brothers, A Bug's Life, and Ratatouille?* More recently we have enjoyed *Megan Leavey, The Angry Bird's Movie, The Good Dinosaur,* and *Ferdinand.* Can you name other famous animal movies? What's your favorite?

Documentaries also demonstrate our love for and admiration of animals. Here are just a few from the last 15 years: *Planet Earth, Blackfish, Oceans, March of the Penguins, The Cove, Arctic Tale, In the Valley of the Wolves, Winged Migration, The Last Lions, An Apology to Elephants, Wild Horse, Wild Ride,* and *Unbranded.* We watch because we are hungry to learn more about animals.

We love it when commercials use animals to sell their products. Geico sells their product through a gecko full of personality, deer using night-goggles, and a sloth playing Pictionary, very slowly! Don't you enjoy the Budweiser commercials when the Clydesdales are the stars? Have you laughed at the Chick-Fil-A cows encouraging us to "eat mor chikin"? Do the golden retrievers in the "dog tested, dog approved" commercials make you have a good feeling about Subaru cars? We may not buy the product, but we love the animal-based humor and entertainment! Have you enjoyed other commercials with animals?

Animals are frequently in the news. For example, in the months before the writing of this book, I read stories or watched videos about (1) men going out on thin ice and risking their lives to save some elk which had fallen into the freezing water, (2) a man stopping on the highway to help a wild baby horse get over a fence and join its mother, (3) people flocking to beaches to aid whales which had sadly beached themselves, and (4) fishermen pulling a drowning herd of deer onto their boat and safely releasing them on the shore. Because we humans are often willing to take risks to save even wild animals, we regularly see stories like this in the news.

On the web, many news sites have a special section of video clips about animals. Do you know why? News bosses know these visual stories will increase the number of hits on their website, because we love watching them.

Animals Abound in Our Community Life

Think about how our communities are overflowing with animal shelters, animal rescue groups, and animal adoption agencies. Most are run by volunteers who are passionate about animals. Abundant are the groups which specialize in promoting animal rights and saving endangered species.

We have animal hospitals, animal doctors, and animal medical procedures and medicines. Because we love our animals, we spend a lot of money on them. According to the American Pet Products Association website, in the U.S. alone, we spent $72.56 billion (not million) on our pets in 2018![1] This includes $2.01 billion on live animal purchases, $30.32 billion for pet food, $16.01 billion on pet supplies and medicines, $18.11 billion at the vet, and $6.11 billion on grooming and boarding our pets. Think about it. That's a lot of money! That's a lot of love!

Because of our fascination with animals, we flock to zoos and other types of animal parks. There are thousands of zoos and aquariums around the world. Did you know that April 8 is National Zoo Lover's Day? The World Association of Zoos and Aquariums reports having over 700 million visitors per year.[2] While there, we ooh and aw at the beauty, power, speed, cuteness or intelligence of each animal.

I could go on, but I think the fact is clear. Humans love and admire animals. The bond between the two runs deep.

Animals Love and Admire Humans

My friend Louie is a Marine who struggles with depression related to PTSD. He used to have a comfort dog named Emmett.

Once when Louie and Emmett were home alone, Louie was in the bedroom with the door partially closed. In the depths of despair, Louie didn't think he could take it anymore. He sat on the bed, put his .38 to his temple, and released the safety device. Just as he was about to pull the trigger, Emmett pushed the door open, jumped up on the bed, and lay his head on Louie's shoulder, whimpering. How could Emmett have understood what was happening? How did he know the way to stop the suicide of the human he loved? We don't know. What we do know is that Louie changed his mind. Emmett's love helped him realize that life was worth living.

On August 16, 1996, Chicago local news stations carried the story of a three-year old boy who fell into the Brookfield Zoo gorilla enclosure and lay there unconscious.[3] A female gorilla named Binti Jua quickly came to the boy's rescue, cradling him in her arms and protecting him from the other gorillas, while carrying her own baby on her back. The female carried the little boy about 60 feet to a door where she handed him to zoo workers. The little boy recovered from the injuries related to his fall. Binti Jua had been abandoned as a baby and partially raised by humans. She had developed a respect for humans which led her to save the little boy!

I went to the baptism party of a two-year-old girl named Kennedy. I had never been to her house, but her father had told me about their Great Dane named Athena. After meeting Kennedy's family, I noticed something astonishing through the sliding glass doors to the backyard patio. Huge Athena was sitting very still as four little girls were dressing her in their doll clothes. Why would this huge animal let these little girls have so much fun with her? The answer is clear. Athena loved them!

Throughout history, dolphins have been known to be supportive and helpful to humans. In August of 2000, off the coast of Manfredonia, Italy, in the Adriatic Sea, a 14-year-old boy fell off his family's boat.[4] The boy couldn't swim and began to sink. In the area lived a bottlenose dolphin that had been separated from a visiting school of dolphins. He had become an interesting tourist attraction and had been given the name Filippo. Filippo happened to see the drowning boy, swam under him, lifted him to the surface, and carried him to a nearby boat. This dolphin is a special example of the concern these animals sometimes show for humans.

When we lived in Venezuela, we had a beautiful boxer named Becky. We got her about a year before our third child, David, was born. When David was brought home from the hospital, Becky seemed to think this new, human baby was her pup. She begged to smell and kiss David. When he was old enough to sit up, Becky was always sitting next to him. Later, while he played in the yard, Becky stayed within a foot of him. It appeared that her mission in life was to protect this little human being with a loving and caring attitude.

Becky loved me, too. I often arrived home late at night after my wife and kids were asleep. In her excitement to see me, Becky always carried out a routine in which she would run a lap around the front yard at break-neck speed, do a few circles around me, then as I knelt, lunge at me, nose-first. We would wrestle for a bit in the grass before I brought out treats, putting half the popcorn in her food bowl, and half the beer in her water bowl. She scarfed them down without stopping to breathe, and after a loud burp, would sit on my lap for some relaxing conversation. It's very fulfilling to be loved by such an animal!

You may also have stories of how animals show their love, comfort and protection to the humans in their lives. It is simply a fact of life.

Why All This Love between Humans and Animals?

That we humans share a deep, mutual bond with the animal world is, as we have shown, easily recognized by most people. But we seldom think and talk about why this is so. Why do many animals love us, showing their affection and protection? Conversely, why do we love and admire animals so much?

This book attempts to answer to these questions. I will do this from a Biblical, creationist point of view. Even if you don't believe in the Bible or creation, but love animals and are interested in understanding more about our amazing bond with them, you will love this book. The answers that I provide are based not only on the Bible, but also on human logic and scientific evidence.

First is the question of why animals so often show love and compassion to us humans. I believe that many animals shower us with care and love because they were created by God for this purpose. As we will see in Chapter 1, God created animals before He created humans. This was so that right from the start, the animal kingdom would be available for man's pleasure and companionship. Chapter 4 explains that God loves to use animals for His purposes in this world, including providing care, companionship, and healing to humans. It is no accident that so many animals bond with us. It is by design: God's design.

Second is the question of why we humans love and admire animals so strongly. I believe this is because we are created "in God's image" (Genesis 1:26-27). By that I mean that we were created in such a way that we naturally reflect or mirror some of the characteristics of the God who created us. Since the fall into sin, as recorded in Genesis 3, we no longer reflect God's characteristics all the time. In fact, in many cases, our behavior is the polar-opposite of who God is. But the fact remains that much of what we love and care about is a reflection of the image of God in us. Here are a few examples: When we care about justice it is because God is just. We love variety, beauty, and order because God loves variety, beauty, and order. We appreciate creativity, art, and engineering because God is the ultimate Creator, Artist, and Engineer. When we admire kindness and helpfulness it is because God is kind and helpful.

God loves and admires animals, and since we are made in His image, we also love and admire them. If this is true, we have not only answered the question of why we love animals but have also provided the basis for appreciating more than ever our bond with them. We know this bond is not by accident, but by design: God's design!

But how can we be sure that God loves animals? I will show

six ways in which He demonstrates His love for them. We may love animals, but our love for them pales in comparison to God's radical love for the animal kingdom. So, let's see if it's true. Is God really *The Greatest Animal Lover?*

CHAPTER 1

CREATION

Introduction

Can you imagine what Planet Earth was like on the morning of day five of Creation before God created the animal kingdom? If you were swimming or snorkeling in your favorite lake, river or ocean, you wouldn't have seen fish, dolphins, lobsters, oysters, or sea urchins. God designed the waters to be the favorite playground of aquatic animals, but up to this point, the waters, sadly, had no animal life.

If you were hiking in a grass-covered valley, and looked up into the sky, you wouldn't have seen a single bird, butterfly, bee, dragonfly, or bat. Even though God designed the air to be the perfect habitat for animals that fly, the air, sadly, was empty of flying creatures.

If you were climbing a mountain and looking through your binoculars to scan the nearby valleys, plains, and mountains, you would not have seen land animals - horses, dogs, elephants, rabbits, bighorn sheep, mountain lions, or squirrels. God designed the dry land to be the perfect home for animals that run, climb, and burrow, but sadly, the land was completely void of them.

Water, air, and land were three beautiful, carefully designed animal environments, but when would they be populated? We have gone back to early on day five of Creation, because the all-powerful, Creator God was about to fill the waters with animals that love to swim (Chapter 1A), and the skies with animals that love to fly (Chapter 1B). On the morning of day six, before creating the human race, He would fill the dry land with animals that love to run, jump, climb, and dig (Chapter 1C). God shows His love for animals in the intricate way He formed each one. Let's look at how the Bible describes the miracle of the creation of animals.

CHAPTER 1A – AQUATIC ANIMALS

In Genesis 1, day five of Creation occupies verses 20 to 23. In these verses, the information about the creation of flying and aquatic animals is mixed together, so for clarity, I have separated what these verses say about the two categories.

Here is what Genesis 1:20-23 says about the creation of animals that love to swim:

> [20]"*Let the waters teem with living creatures* . . . [21]*So God created the great creatures of the sea, and every living and moving thing with which the water teems, according to their kinds* . . . *and God saw that it was good* . . . [22]*And God blessed them and said, "Be fruitful and increase in number and fill the water in the seas* . . . [23]*and there was evening and there was morning, the fifth day.*"

If you love to fish, visit Sea World, go snorkeling, eat shrimp or lobster, keep an aquarium full of fish in your home, or swim with the dolphins, then this moment in creation history is huge for you! With great love and intricate design, God created the aquatic animals. Let's look at a few key terms and concepts from the verses above.

In verse 20, God said, "Let the waters *teem* with living creatures." God didn't want there to be just a few animals that love the water;

He wanted the waters to be brimming with these beautiful creatures. Despite centuries of human abuse, the superabundance of water animals is still true today! As of 2019, there are over 30,000 species of fish[5], about 70,000 species of crustaceans[6], and about 130 species of aquatic mammals![7] The number of species of each type of marine animal is in a continual upward swing, as more species are discovered by marine biologists. This plethora of swimming animals can also be measured by the size of the schools in which they swim. Some chains of schools can be up to 60 miles long. Herring often school densely, with up to three billion fish in a cubic mile of the ocean.[8] God must love it; the waters are still "teeming" with animal life!

Verse 21 says that God "created the *great* creatures of the sea," referring to the extremely large animals that live in water. The largest known creature is the blue whale, which can be up to 100 feet long (three times as long as the famous orcas) and weigh up to 400,000 pounds, or about 200 tons![9] Another "great creature of the sea" is the giant squid, the largest invertebrate known to man, which can grow up to 60 feet long and weigh over a ton. God delighted in making the huge marine animals, and He enjoys it when we are impressed with their size today.

Verse 21 also says that God created "*every* living and moving thing with which the water teems." He certainly created a vast array of animals that love to swim and live in water! Debbie and Richard Lawrence delineate this variety in the following order.[10]

Perhaps God started by creating the fish. These abundant, cold-blooded, gill-breathing, egg-laying vertebrates are designed for speed-swimming in the water. God gave most fish scales, all of which point back toward their tail, allowing the water to flow smoothly over and around them. They have glands under their scales that secrete a slimy mucus making them slick for quicker movement in the water. For powerful locomotion, God gave fish fins - lots of fins: pectoral fins on the sides of their bodies near the front, pelvic fins lower and farther back, dorsal and anal fins on the top and bottom, and the caudal fin at the end of their tails. Each kind of fin plays a unique role in propelling and balancing the fish through the water. God's design for most fish also includes a swim bladder, a balloon-like sac that can be inflated or deflated to help the fish rise or go deeper in the water, as well as a special respiratory system of gills that grab oxygen from water like our lungs do from air. But God made gills very efficient because He knew that swimming burns lots of energy.

So please think this through for a moment. Fish have scales, fins, swim bladders, and gills, all of which are crucial to enjoying life in the water. Might these be "adaptations," which came about through accidental mutations with no direction, guidance, or purpose? To me, they sound like parts of an anatomy designed by a loving and brilliant Designer. What do you think?

Since God loves variety, He also designed some fish to have cartilage structures instead of a bony skeleton. There are over 1,000 known species of cartilaginous fish[11], including rays, lampreys, hagfish, and the most famous of all, the intriguing shark. Sharks don't have swim bladders, so if they stop swimming, they sink to the bottom, which is why momma sharks are always telling their babies, "Swim or sink, Honey, swim or sink." Their gill structure and function are also different from bony fish. Even more surprising, most sharks give birth to live babies instead of laying eggs, but they still belong to the fish family!

If God started creating marine life with the fish, He was just getting warmed up! Perhaps next He created the crustaceans, which are egg-laying invertebrates with jointed feet, segmented bodies, and exoskeletons designed to live in the water. The crustaceans include shrimp, crabs, lobsters, crawdads, and teeny-tiny brine shrimp and water fleas. God designed them with two distinct body parts (the cephalothorax and the abdomen), two pairs of antennae, two or more pairs of legs, and gills for breathing in the water. They are also delicious and nutritious!

Possibly after seeing the magnificence of the fish and crustaceans, God decided to create the mollusks. These amazing aquatic invertebrates have their own God-given design. Their soft, boneless, unsegmented bodies consist of one muscular foot, a mantle, and a hump that contains the vital organs. The mantle secretes a substance which hardens into a shell, so yes, we are talking about shellfish. There are three main kinds of mollusks. First, the bivalves, such as clams and oysters, have a two-part shell connected by a hinge and produce a pearly substance as they grow. Second, the gastropods, each species of which produces a uniquely spiraled, one-piece shell, include snails, conchs, abalones, and slugs. Third, the cephalopods, including squids, octopuses, and nautiluses, show us God's sense of humor. In addition to a hump and a mantle, cephalopods have a foot merged with the head! God gave squids and octopuses advantageous characteristics such as a water-based jet propulsion system to speed through the water, and the ability to shoot out an inky substance to confuse their predators. The complex eye of the octopus has much in common with the human eye, and its intricate brain makes it one of the most intelligent invertebrates. Each mollusk is fascinating and brilliantly designed to enjoy life in the water.

Wow . . . fish, crustaceans, mollusks! Was God satisfied with this variety of water animals? Not even close! Perhaps next He made the cnidarians, such as jellyfish, coral, and sea anemones, which have hollow bodies and stinging tentacles. The Portuguese man-of-war also belongs to this group, but he is a siphonophore, which means a collection of cnidarians living in a symbiotic relationship. Complex design for life in the water!

Possibly God chose to create the echinoderms next. These spiny-skinned marine animals with hard spikes made from calcium carbonate propel themselves by means of a complex system of water-filled tubes called the water vascular system. Most echinoderms have a central disk from which five to ten rays protrude. You may be guessing some of the famous members of this group, which include the starfish, sea urchins, and sand dollars.

Several features of starfish capture our attention. Though we wouldn't expect it, they can move quickly along the seafloor. Their diet consists mainly of bivalve clams and oysters. They pry open the oyster's shell with their arms, force their stomach through their mouth into the shell, partially digest their prey, and then pull their stomach back into their body. Not pretty, but very effective. Another awesome trait of the starfish is that it can regenerate missing body parts! Every type of aquatic animal is evidence of God's brilliant design.

God also created <u>sponges</u> to love life in the ocean. At first glance, they seem more like plants than animals, but not so. In their larva stage, they move around (plants don't travel), but as adults they anchor themselves on the ocean floor. Sponges extract oxygen and microscopic organisms from the water that flows through their many pores. Waste products are released through an opening at the top of their body. They like to live near coral and sometimes overtake a coral colony. They are harvested for use as cleaning tools. God must love variety!

God also decided to create <u>aquatic worms</u>, such as the giant tube worm, which lives near hydrothermal vents on the floor of the Pacific Ocean. Growing up to eight feet long, tube worms love life in this almost boiling, chemically toxic water, where most animals would die. From the black water, they absorb oxygen, hydrogen sulfide, and carbon dioxide which bacteria convert into carbohydrates for food through a complex digestive process called chemosynthesis. This is another brilliant design by the Creator for a marine animal which loves life in a place where few dare to go.

God probably also created the <u>aquatic mammals</u> at this time. Humans have a special fascination with these animals and love to learn about dolphins, porpoises, manatees, whales, seals, sea lions, and walruses. We marvel that they breathe through their lungs like we do, yet God obviously designed them to enjoy life in the water.

Dolphins, porpoises, and whales all have powerful tail fins called flukes. While the tail fins of fish move from side to side, flukes move up and down. They are so effective that some dolphins can swim up to 25 miles per hour!

Since they are designed to live in the water, these aquatic mammals don't breathe through noses like land mammals; they breathe through a blowhole, an opening at the top of their heads. They can hold their breath for a long time: porpoises for about four minutes, dolphins for about eight to fifteen minutes, and the sperm whale for an hour or more. The sperm whale is designed to be the king of diving, even to a depth of more than 4,000 feet where he eats his favorite meal, the giant squid![12]

Of God's created aquatic animals, we have mentioned fish, crustaceans, mollusks, cnidarians, echinoderms, sponges, worms, and aquatic mammals. This is just a partial list since we haven't described many others like the aquatic reptiles, which include snakes, turtles, and crocodiles. But we have seen a master Designer who loves variety and beauty in the water. He nailed it when He created "every living and moving thing with which the water teems!" God, *The Greatest Animal Lover*, loves and admires His aquatic animals.

CHAPTER 1B – FLYING ANIMALS

Here is what Genesis 1:20-23 says about the creation of animals that love to fly:

> [20]*"And let birds fly above the earth across the expanse of the sky . . .* [21]*So God created . . . every winged bird according to its kind . . . And God saw that it was good . . .* [22]*God blessed them and said, "Be fruitful and increase in number . . . and let the birds increase on the earth.* [23]*And there was evening and there was morning, the fifth day."*

I love what God says at the beginning of verse 20, "And let the birds fly!" I'm sure it was fun for God to create the animals that love to swim in the water which He designed for them, but these words give us insight into the excitement God felt when He created animals that love to fly through the air. One of the reasons He created Earth's atmosphere was so that winged animals could enjoy flying in it. We are fascinated by flight because the image of the God who created it is in us.

Birds

As you can imagine, creating animals that fly in the air required a very different design than animals which swim in water or walk on dry land. But God is the Master Designer of flight, and He thought of everything. First, He designed a different bone structure for birds. Most bird bones are partially hollow to reduce weight and reinforced with struts to make them amazingly strong. Second, He gave birds a unique muscle system. The breast muscles, which pull the wings downward, are surprisingly strong and almost tireless, which is crucial for lift. Third, He designed a special respiratory system for birds. Flying burns a lot of energy, so oxygen must be abundant in their bodies. Due to the flow of air through various air sacks and the lungs, birds are able to inhale and exhale twice with each breath of air, getting double the oxygen. Plus, the blood in their lungs is always flowing in the opposite direction of the air flow (called "countercurrent exchange"), resulting in the greatest possible intake of oxygen. This is how birds take in more oxygen than most animals. Fourth, God designed birds to be covered with feathers of which there are three different kinds. Down feathers provide insulation near the bird's body. Over these are the contour feathers, all of which point towards the tail so that air can flow smoothly over its body. Finally, the wings are covered with a variety of flight feathers. A hook and barb system keeps these feathers in the best position for efficient flight, while the bird's tail serves as a rudder. Fifth, God put into most birds' DNA a powerful GPS system, which is vital for their migratory practice. The arctic tern is the king of migration. Many terns have their nesting grounds up in the Arctic, only to travel about 12,000 miles south to enjoy the Antarctic summer. Year after year, they easily find their same Arctic and Antarctic "neighborhoods," and never get lost! When you put together hollow, strutted bones, powerful breast muscles, a super-efficient respiratory system, a complex combination of feathers, and an accurate GPS system, you have a lean, mean flying machine, just as God designed it.

In verse 21, the phrase, "so God created . . . *every* winged bird . . ." is important because He created many kinds. Most ornithologists estimate that there are between 10,000 and 11,000 species of birds on our planet, though some specialists, by tweaking the meaning of "species," now calculate more than 18,000![13] Either way, that's a lot of kinds of birds! There are many ways to put birds into groups. As with the water animals, I like the way Debbie and Richard Lawrence categorize them.[14]

First, there are <u>perching</u> birds, which generally have three toes facing forward and one backward for grasping branches. Perching birds include songbirds, such as the thrush, robin, whippoorwill, mockingbird, bluebird, and sparrow. The gift of music, which God put into the songbird DNA, is phenomenal indeed! The other day my grandson and I were listening to a mockingbird in the front yard. Within about three minutes, we heard it sing 15 distinct mini songs. Song bird researchers are now transcribing bird songs onto musical signatures. Many songbirds, such as the musician wren, sing songs with striking similarities to human compositions![15]

Among the perching birds are the beloved hummingbirds. Though not blessed with song, they are extremely gifted, miniature flying machines. To get into their world, try to imagine their tiny heart beating up to 1,200 times per minute and their little wings flapping 80 times per second, as they visit up to 1,000 flowers per day. They can fly in a straight line at 30 miles per hour and dive at up to 60 miles per hour. They can hover, fly backwards and upside down, and make it look easy. Their beautiful iridescent colors continually wow us. Wherever on the planet these little birds are found, humans gaze in awe. I can't help but think that even though God is proud of all His created birds, He is especially proud of the little hummingbird.

Another songless perching bird which captures our attention is the woodpecker. It seems that woodpeckers should suffer from concussions and brain damage in general. They peck tree trunks about 8,000 to 12,000 times a day, whether hunting for insects, excavating for a nest, or attracting a mate. With each peck, their head/beak is ramming into solid wood at 12 or 13 miles per hour. But they don't suffer brain damage or even get headaches! God designed them with specialized headgear which prevents damage to their brain and eyes. The woodpecker's skull bone is spongy at the forehead and the back of the skull, so with every peck, it serves as a shock absorber. Also, just before its beak strikes the tree trunk, nictitating membranes close over its eyes, providing protection from the flying debris caused by the blow of its beak against the wood. God designed the woodpecker not only to safely enjoy flight, but also pecking!

A second category of birds, famous for their speed and accuracy, are the birds of prey, including eagles, hawks, falcons, and owls. They are known for their keen eyesight, hooked beaks, and sharp talons, all used for catching and killing their prey. God gave the bald eagle astonishing vision, able to spot small prey from up to two miles away! Hawks are both fearless and ferocious hunters. The red-tailed hawk loves to attack and make a meal of rattlesnakes! The peregrine falcon is known as the fastest member of the animal kingdom. During a hunting stoop (high speed dive), it can speed downward at over 200 miles per hour! Many owls have a sense of hearing which boggles our minds. From far away, the great gray owl can hear the rustling of a mouse or lemming tunneling under six to twelve inches of snow. He dives talon first into the snow and catches his unsuspecting prey. Humans are always impressed with these birds. Their highly developed senses of sight and sound and their impressive flying acrobatics remind us of their Designer and Creator!

Third, is a group of birds that are just as at home in the water as they are in the air. How lucky are they? The waterfowl include geese, ducks, and swans. Canada geese have been known to fly as high as 9,000 feet, but they love to land on or near water. They are good swimmers and enjoy eating aquatic plants. Ducks also fly and swim with ease, but in addition, skillfully dive for their tasty meals. The long-tailed duck can dive 200 feet below the surface. Isn't it surprising that they can hold their breath that long and not be crushed by the water pressure? God designed some birds to both fly high in the air and dive deep in the water.

Fourth, are birds which taste especially good. The game birds include wild turkey, pheasant, and quail. The pheasant is more colorful than the quail, but both are beautiful. The quail has a cute plume on its head which bobs as he walks. None of these birds fly for long distances, which makes them easier to hunt. They are tasty and nourishing.

Fifth, are birds known for their stark beauty. The <u>tropical birds</u> include parrots, parakeets, toucans, and many more. We can't get enough of their bright blacks, blues, greens, reds, yellows, and oranges. We are impressed and entertained when they learn to imitate human speech. Some of them make great pets. When we lived in Caracas, we shopped at a little grocery store whose owner had a beautiful macaw that greeted us as we entered the shop. When the owner ran his errands on a motor scooter, the macaw flew about two feet above his shoulder and landed on it at stop signs. We felt fortunate when we were driving behind the owner and his macaw, getting to observe the stark beauty of the bird and the deep bond with its owner.

Finally, though it may sound like a contradiction, there are <u>flightless</u> birds. These include the ostrich, emu, rhea, cassowary, kiwi, and penguin. The ostrich, the largest bird on earth today, grows up to nine feet tall and weighs up to 300 pounds. It may not be able to fly, but God designed it to run up to 45 miles per hour. In the wilds of Africa, imagine all the ostrich predators lying in the grass frustrated, out of breath, and hungry!

It is interesting that the flightless penguin could also be included in the water fowl mentioned above. There are about 17 species of penguins and all of them live along coastal areas and love the water.[16] On land, penguins waddle and look rather clumsy. Some say that the penguin's wings are useless, but this is far from true. The wings serve as flippers which propel the bird through the water with such speed and grace that it appears to be flying underwater.

This is only an abbreviated list of the kinds of birds God created to enjoy flight, and a few which prefer solid ground or life in the water. You may be frustrated because I left out your favorite bird, for which I'm sorry, but this brief overview helps us get a perspective of the great variety of birds God designed and created for our pleasure.

Mammals

Though the Genesis Creation account only specifically names birds, it is probable that at this time God also created other kinds of animals that enjoy flight. To our knowledge, one mammal loves to fly through the air: the bat, of which there are about 1,240 known species![17] Bats are unusual mammals, and though they fly, they are different from birds. They have hair, not feathers, and what appear to be wings are more like hands with long fingers that have leathery skin stretched over them.

There are two main kinds of bats: megabats and microbats. Megabats are generally larger and eat fruit and nectar. Most have strong senses of sight and sound. Hundreds of types of flowering plants depend on megabats for pollination. Microbats are generally smaller and eat insects. They spot their prey and navigate dark caves by echolocation. As they fly they send out high-pitched sound waves, which hit an object and bounce back (echo) to them, informing them of the exact location of the object, even if it's tiny and moving. Many microbats eat up to 1,000 mosquitoes per hour, using echolocation and a remarkable ability to turn quickly in flight. Let's lift our glasses and toast these blessed creatures! These mammalian flying machines are not just interesting, they are also of great value.

Insects

What about all the insects that love to fly? Since they are blessed with flight, God may have created them in the same time frame as the birds. Though they are born mostly as water or land animals, in adulthood they basically live in the air. Some flying insects go through a three-step metamorphosis, starting as an egg, advancing to a nymph, and finishing as an adult. The beautiful and fascinating dragonflies are an example. They spend most of their lives in water as nymphs, eating and molting. When they are ready to begin their adult lives as dragonflies, they crawl out of the water and undergo the last stage of their metamorphosis. When completed, they have two large compound eyes that have up to 30,000 lenses and almost a 360-degree vision! Their two sets of wings (total of 4) enable them to hover and fly up, down, forward and backward. They can fly up to 30 miles per hour and make high-speed hairpin turns. If this weren't enough, they are also blessed with beautiful colors. Another special design by the Creator of flight!

But most flying insects go through a four-step metamorphosis. They start as an egg, become a larva, advance to a chrysalis (pupa), and finish as an adult. Butterflies are an example. Have you been to a butterfly habitat lately? My wife and I did while I was writing this book and we enjoyed it so much we went through a second time. Most butterflies live for only two to four weeks. If they get too cold or too hot, they can't fly and become an easy meal for their predators. So sad. Their delicate wings are made of transparent layers of chitin, covered with tiny scales which reflect light in different colors. They have no chewing mechanism, so they enjoy a pure liquid diet which they drink through their straw-like, tubular tongue (proboscis). There is nothing simplistic about the design of a butterfly. The female has chemoreceptors on the spines at the back of her legs so she can find the right plant on which to lay her eggs! We mostly love butterflies for their light-hearted flight and their colorful beauty.

We have looked at just a few of the birds, mammals and insects which God designed for flight and created on day five of Creation. What a Master Creator and Lover of animals He is! I'm so glad He created animals which love to fly. How about you?

CHAPTER 1C – LAND ANIMALS

Day five of Creation had been amazing. At God's command, there was an explosion of animal life. The rivers, lakes, oceans, and seas of Planet Earth were now teeming with aquatic animals. The atmosphere was now crowded with animals which love to fly. However, the third habitat, the dry land which God had also designed for life, was still empty. But not for long!

During the first part of day six of Creation, God mainly created animals that delight in running, jumping, and burrowing on dry land. Here is what Genesis 1:24-25 says about the creation of animals that enjoy life on solid ground:

> [24]And God said, "Let the land produce living creatures according to their kinds: livestock, creatures that move along the ground, and wild animals, each according to its kind." And it was so. [25]God made the wild animals according to their kinds, the livestock according to their kinds, and all the creatures that move along the ground according to their kinds. And God saw that it was good."

Verse 24 says, "Let the land produce living creatures." This probably means that in some way God used the soil in the process of creating the land animals. We don't know the details. In Chapter 2:7 we read that God "formed the man from the dust of the ground." In 2:19 we read that God "formed out of the ground all the beasts of the field and all the birds of the air." How He did this we don't know; but God used the dirt as He went about creating the animals and even man himself.

Verse 25 gives us a good summary of what kinds of animals God created on the first part of day six. "God made the wild animals according to their kinds, the livestock according to their kinds, and all the creatures that move along the ground according to their kinds." Let's think about these day six animals. As in the case of the aquatic and flying animals, we will follow the way that Debbie and Richard Lawrence present the land animals.[18]

Mammals

Many of the best-known land animals are mammals. God created mammals with five main characteristics. First, they are warm-blooded which means that their metabolism enables them to maintain a constant body temperature regardless of the temperature of the surrounding environment. Second, they have hair or fur, not scales or feathers. Third, with few exceptions, they give birth to live babies as opposed to laying eggs. Fourth, females feed milk to their young through distinct mammary glands. Fifth, they breathe air through lungs, not gills or spores. Though almost all mammals share these characteristics designed by God, there are still many different kinds of mammals.

As we focus on the mammals that God created to enjoy life on dry land, we won't talk about two kinds of mammals. The aquatic mammals such as dolphins, porpoises, whales, sea cows, seals, sea lions, and walruses were probably created on day five with all the animals that love life in the water. Similarly, the bat was probably created on day five with all the animals to which God gave the gift of flight.

Large Mammals

One group of mammals could be called the "large ones," and includes the elephants, giraffes, bears, rhinoceros, hippopotami, etc. God, who loves variety, must have had fun designing these big ones. And He probably enjoys it when we are in awe of their hugeness!

Elephants are the largest known land mammals. Some can stand ten feet tall and weigh up to six tons. God gave elephants a trunk with over 40,000 muscles, while the entire human body only has about 640! This is why the trunk is so versatile and powerful. Since some areas of their skin can be up to an inch thick, elephants are called pachyderms, which means "thick-skinned." They can flap their extra-large ears to keep cool on a hot day. Fatty tissue enables their feet to serve as shock absorbers for a very heavy animal. They have large brains and can communicate in multiple ways. No wonder elephants delight us!

Many bears are also huge animals. The grizzly, Alaskan brown, and polar bears weigh between 800 and 1,700 pounds and standing on their hind legs can reach eight to ten feet. Their size is of course one of the reasons we humans feel fear at the thought of being confronted by a bear. There are only eight known types of bear, and all share many of the same characteristics. They live solitary lives, hibernate in the winter, and enjoy communicating with about seven or eight specific vocal pronouncements.

The tallest known land mammal is the giraffe, standing up to 19 or 20 feet tall. This is amazing considering that the height of a standard basketball hoop is only ten feet. The giraffe's neck alone can be up to six or seven feet long. This is advantageous when it wants to eat some delicious leaves off the top of trees, but potentially dangerous when it needs to lower its head to quench its thirst. The risk is double: as it lowers its head the brain could be flooded with blood, and when it raises its head, the brain could be left with insufficient blood. But neither problem occurs because God gave giraffes a marvelous circulatory system. Between their heart and head, giraffes have a blood pressure regulation system consisting of a super-strong heart, a network of valves, and specialized blood vessels. Those long giraffe legs also have an extraordinary circulatory design. They are wrapped with extremely tight skin which helps the blood pressure stay strong as the blood makes the lengthy return trip up the legs. Some might think giraffes are too tall for their own good. This isn't true because God designed them to have a great life in their very tall bodies!

Small Mammals

A broad group of small mammals includes pika, mice, voles, hamsters, and gerbils. Though our planet is covered with thousands of kinds of small mammals, two have managed to work their way into our homes as pets: hamsters and gerbils. In the wild, hamsters are crepuscular, which means they are most active in the twilight hours. The adult Roborovski dwarf hamster is only about two inches long, while the European hamster can grow up to thirteen inches. God gave them cheek pouches where they can store a meal for later. An average litter size is seven babies, but some hamsters are known to deliver up to twenty-four! Hamsters only live an average of two and a half years, so owners and pets need to make the most of their time together! Gerbils, with their long hind legs, love to burrow, which is why in the wild they create extensive networks of tunnels. They are smart and social, so it's best for them to have other gerbils as cage-mates. They delight in hoarding food and gnawing continually. Gerbil fathers are very involved in raising their babies. It is a beautiful thing that millions of families welcome these and other small, God-created mammals as their house pets.

Ruminants

God also created the ruminants which have always been of great importance to humans for transportation, farming, pets, skins, wool, meat, and milk. Cows, goats, sheep, buffalo, moose, elk, antelopes, giraffes, camels, oxen, and deer all form part of this group. Some of these are described in verse 25 which says that God "made the livestock according to their kinds." Since they love to eat grass, hay, and many other plants which are hard to digest, ruminants need a brilliant digestive system, so that's just what God gave them.

Here's how these interesting animals digest their grasses and plants: They give the food an initial chew and then send it down to the first chamber (rumen) where serious digestion begins. The food passes to the second chamber (reticulum) for more digestion. It then shoots back up to the mouth for a second chew ("chewing the cud"), before being sent down to chambers three and four (omasum and abomasum) to complete the process of absorbing the nutrients from the food. All through the process, bacteria and digestive juices are doing the job of breaking down the grasses into usable nutrients. What a remarkably designed digestive system for land animals that enjoy eating tough-to-digest plants! It comes as no surprise that the word ruminant means "to chew over again."

Though each ruminant is a fascinating land animal about which we enjoy learning, I have a favorite. I love to hike the desert mountains of southern Nevada and am blessed when I see the bighorn sheep. With their split hooves and strong sense of balance, they can easily navigate ledges only two inches wide! They sprint up near-vertical cliffs, and at the top often stop and look back at me, as if to say, "Bet you can't do that!" Of course I can't, but they were specifically designed to thrive and love life in the rugged desert mountains.

Marsupials

God also created the marsupials which means "pouched." This fascinating group includes kangaroos, koalas, numbats, mulgaras, and Tasmanian devils. Today there are more than 295 known species of marsupials, most of which live in or near Australia.[19] One interesting design component in marsupials is that their babies (called joeys) are born very early in their development and migrate to the safety of their mother's pouch, where they can feast on their mother's milk.

The most famous of the marsupials is the kangaroo which comes in all sizes. The musky rat kangaroo is only about a foot tall, while the red kangaroo can grow to eight feet. These big guys can hop at speeds up to 35 miles per hour and jump 30 feet in a single leap! Just as God designed fish for swimming and birds for flying, He gave kangaroos a special design for hopping. First, they have a big middle toe on each foot which helps them push off with each hop. Second, they have large tails which aid them in keeping their balance at high speeds. Third, they have a special tendon at the back of each leg which stores energy in between hops and releases energy when their feet hit the ground. Incredible, right? Their Creator fashioned them to be hopping machines!

Primates

God also enjoyed creating the primates. There are three categories of primates: monkeys, apes, and prosimians. God's design for primates includes ten fingers and ten toes. Their eyes are on the front of their faces which allows them to have very good depth perception.

The largest group of primates is <u>monkeys</u>, of which there are about 260 species.[20] Some are tiny like the pygmy marmoset, while others are large like the mandrill. Most monkeys spend much of their lives in trees and are mainly herbivores. Old World monkeys live in Africa and Asia and tend to be larger than New World monkeys which live in Central and South America. Though all monkeys have tails, the western hemisphere monkeys are blessed with a prehensile tail, with which they easily grasp branches. This makes them excellent tree climbers and swingers.

A second group of primates is <u>apes</u>. They are smaller in number but larger in size than monkeys. They don't have tails, but like monkeys they tend to walk using their knuckles. God designed them to love life in the tropical forests of Africa and Southeast Asia. Four of the better-known apes are the gorilla, the chimpanzee, the orangutan, and the gibbon. Gorillas are famous for their strength, which is equal to about six to eight men! (I hope you enjoyed the true story of Binti Jua in the Introduction!) Chimpanzees are social, intelligent, and live 50 to 60 years! Orangutans are the largest of any animal which enjoys life in trees. Gibbons are the speed demons of the apes, able to brachiate (swing from branch to branch) at speeds up to 35 miles per hour!

The idea that humans have evolved from apes is highly unlikely. First, each supposed example of "missing links" has been proven to be 100% human, 100% ape, or an outright fraud. Second, we see no current examples of apes evolving into humans. Third, apes obviously possess none of the DNA necessary to build the intellect and communication skills of humans. The Bible is right: humans are not animals; rather we are a different category of being, created "in the image of God" (Genesis 1:26-27).

A third category of primates is <u>prosimians</u>. These small animals don't look like monkeys or apes, but they share the primate characteristics of ten fingers, ten toes and binocular vision. Most prosimians live on the island of Madagascar. This group includes lemurs, tarsiers, lorises, and bush babies. Once again, we see God's love of variety!

Man's Favorite Mammals

For many humans, there is a group of mammals which we can simply call our favorites. It includes dogs, cats, and horses.

Dogs aren't called "man's best friend" for nothing. Besides the fact that dogs are so loving, caring, and loyal that we consider them part of the family, God gave them intriguing traits. Their senses of hearing, sight, and smell are much better than ours. In general, their intelligence compares to a two-year-old child. They can read their owner's emotions. Think about how amazing that is! We saw examples of this in the Introduction and in Chapter 4 we'll see that dogs can also help people with a wide array of health problems.

Cats also have proven to be our good friends. Many of us love our smaller house cats despite their super-independent attitude. If a dog's attitude communicates to its owner, "I'm so lucky to belong to you," a cat says, "You're so lucky to have me as your pet!" Maybe we are attracted to them because they love to play, sleep, cuddle, and purr. We smile when they get stuck up a tree. Their claws and muscle systems are built for climbing up things, but not for climbing down head first. Once up a tree, they have only three options: climb down backwards, jump, or wait for help. Often, they prefer number three!

Though not easily domesticated, big cats also capture our attention. I think God is especially proud of the larger cats He created. He designed them to be phenomenal athletes. Imagine a track meet with all the best animal athletes on the planet. Guess which one would win the 100, 200, and 400-meter races? The answer is the cheetah, that can cruise at about 75 miles per hour for shorter distances! Which one would win the high jump? The answer is the leopard, that would clear the bar at about 18 to 20 feet! Think about that. The most talented humans can high jump only about eight feet! Guess which one would win the long jump? The snow leopard would eke out a victory over the red kangaroo, jumping between 40 and 45 feet!

Which cat do you think would win a wrestling match between the male lion and the Siberian tiger? The answer is not clear. Even though the tiger is larger and stronger, the lion's mane gives it an advantage. The tiger would keep trying to kill the lion by biting its neck, but the thick mane would prevent the tiger's teeth from penetrating its skin. Instead of a kill, he would keep getting hairballs! Even so, both cats are impressively strong fighters.

If you would like to see the warmhearted side of big cats, watch the YouTube video, "The Lion Whisperer, Kevin Richardson." The profound acceptance and affection shown by these animals is truly surprising.

God created the horse to become one of the most significant animals in the lives of humans. For thousands of years, horses have aided humans with transportation, farming, war, entertainment, friendship, and more. They have large brains, and powerful senses of hearing, smell, sight, and touch. One helpful trait is that they can sleep either lying down or standing up! With their long, powerful legs and their shock absorber hooves, God designed them to be running machines. Since donkeys and zebras are of the same "kind" or family, they are able to interbreed, producing zorses and zedonks! As we will see in Chapter 4, horses were designed by God to enrich human life in many ways.

Amphibians and Reptiles

When Genesis 1:25 says that God created "all the animals that move along the ground," this may refer in part to amphibians and reptiles. God designed amphibians with a specific set of characteristics. They are cold-blooded; have smooth, moist skin; and lay eggs. As they metamorphose from being water creatures to land creatures ("amphibian" means "on both sides of life"), their respiratory system changes from gills to lungs. Imagine the astounding DNA which makes this double respiratory system possible! Today there are over 7,000 species of amphibians.[21] Some of the best-known amphibians are frogs and toads, salamanders, and caecilians. Frogs love to croak for many reasons, one being to find a mate. Each species of frog croaks at a different frequency, so Miss Bullfrog will never respond to Mr. Tree Frog's call. Good thing, huh? Frogs have smoother and moister skin than toads. Salamanders are nocturnal, and some have tongues longer than their bodies while others can grow up to five feet in length. Caecilians are limbless, look like worms, and spend most of their lives burrowing underground. You might think they live in Sicily; but no, they live in South America, Africa and Southeast Asia.

God lovingly created reptiles with their own characteristics. They are cold-blooded, have dry, scaly skin, and lay eggs. Reptiles do not metamorphose like amphibians. They breathe with lungs and have nictitating membranes over their eyes for added protection. (Remember from Chapter 1B that many woodpeckers also have nictitating membranes.) Today there are about 10,700 known species of reptiles.[22] The main categories of reptiles include snakes, lizards, turtles, and crocodiles.

God's design for snakes is elaborate. Think about this. They sense movement vibrations through their lower jaw, perceive scent particles with their tongue, can disconnect their lower jaws from their skull to make their mouth bigger, and though legless, use unique movements to slither along the terrain. Most snakes fall into one of three sub-groups: constrictors, which include pythons and boas; colubrids, which include bull, rat, and garter snakes; and the feared venomous snakes, which include rattlesnakes, coral snakes, and cobras.

Lizards form the largest group of reptiles. We enjoy learning about the iguana, chuckwalla, horned lizard, and chameleon. We know to stay clear of the Gila monster and Komodo dragon.

The gecko of Geico fame has an amazing trait which had puzzled scientists for years. How can it walk upside down on a smooth plate of glass? We now know that the gecko has millions of microscopic hairs (setae) on the bottom of its feet. The end of each hair sub-divides. When dragged along the surface, these setae become powerful suction cups. They can be released as quickly and easily as they are engaged. Today scientists are trying to mimic these gecko hairs to produce new and more effective adhesive surfaces.

There are also abundant species of turtles and tortoises. One of my favorites is the desert tortoise. With its short, strong, scaled front legs, equipped with sharp claws, it is a burrowing machine. Tortoises spend about 95% of their lives underground, including most of November to February. Their burrows can be three to six feet deep and cover more than thirty feet. They can withstand ground temperatures up to 140 degrees and survive a year with no drinking water! The tortoise is truly designed to thrive in the desert.

Before closing our thoughts on reptiles, it is necessary to mention that God also created many different kinds of land-based dinosaurs. Unfortunately, it seems that all of them are now extinct. But thanks to the fossil record, we know that God enjoyed creating a great variety of these remarkable animals.

Insects

Though many insects are gifted with flight, some love living on the ground. Many types of beetles don't fly, so perhaps God created them also on this day six of Creation. With more than 380,000 known species, there are more beetles than any other animal on the planet.[23] As in the case of most insects, beetle DNA guides them through their four-step metamorphosis: egg, larva, pupa, and adult. Beetles enjoy God's brilliant three-body-part anatomical design. The head is their center for communication, with antennae and compound eyes. The thorax is the hub for movement, with three sets of legs and two sets of wings. The abdomen is the location for internal organs and systems.

Beetles come in many sizes. The Titan beetle from South America can grow to eight inches long! Beetle colors are dazzling and can include red, green, yellow, orange, and purple.

One of my favorite land-based beetles is the bombardier beetle. It stores two explosive chemicals in separate interior chambers. When alarmed or threatened, it mixes them in a reservoir where they do not yet explode. When the beetle is ready to fire at its predator, a valve opens, and the gases are transferred into the vestibule where a catalyst causes them to explode at 200 degrees Fahrenheit and blast through an outlet valve, scaring away or killing the enemy. This complex defense mechanism doesn't sound like something which came about in a slow, haphazard way; rather, its Designer must have created all the component parts at once.

Arachnids

God also created the arachnids, or spiders, as part of His day six creation of land animals. Unlike the "three-body-part" design of insects, spiders have a different, yet equally brilliant anatomical design. They have only two body parts, the cephalothorax and the abdomen. They have eight legs but no wings or antennae. God favored some spiders with a silk-spinning organ called the spinneret. A spider's spinnerets are usually found on the underside and to the rear of the abdomen. Most spiders have six spinnerets, but this can vary from two to eight. Scientists are still trying to figure out all the details of how spiders produce and spin silk webs. Some of the strands are smooth and some are sticky. If necessary, the spider can secrete an oily substance from its feet, so it doesn't stick to its own web. The main support for the web is called the dragline, which is many times stronger than an equal amount of steel. Once again, this complex spinning process doesn't sound like it came into being in an unguided, accidental way, but rather by a brilliant Designer.

In concluding this section on the day six creation of land animals, we are impressed with the great variety God brought into being. We have mentioned only a few of the mammals, amphibians, reptiles, insects, and arachnids which God lovingly designed. Each kind of created land animal is a reminder that as their Creator, God truly is *The Greatest Animal Lover!*

CHAPTER 1D – BEHIND THE SCENES

As a result of God's creative activity on days five and six of Creation, the waters were now teeming with all kinds of animals designed to love life in the water. The air was blessed with countless animals designed to enjoy flight. The dry land was active with an abundance of animals designed to be happy on the ground, under the ground, and in the trees. There were and are amazing animals all over the world. But if we only look at and admire the outward appearance of animals, we will be missing much of the phenomenal miracle that each animal represents. Therefore, in this chapter we will go behind the scenes of the creation of the animals in order to appreciate more completely God's great love for each of them. We will look at three of the statements God made about or to the animals as He lovingly created them. Then, we will look at the creation of the animals from the perspective of their systems, cells, and DNA.

"And God saw that it was good." (Genesis 1:21, 25)

With this observation, God was giving His stamp of approval on each of the animals He had created. His compliment in verse 21 is directed at all the flying and swimming animals, and in verse 25, at the land animals. We'll come back to this in just a minute.

If we look at the broader context of the other creation days, we see God giving the very same accolade to each component of His creation. In verse 10, on day three, God concluded that the way He separated the dry land from the gathered waters was a "good" thing. In verse 12, on day three, after having created the various plants, bushes, and trees, God's conclusion was that His created vegetation was indeed "good." On day four, God created Planet Earth's solar system, including our sun, moon, and sister planets with their moons. He then placed our solar system in our galaxy of billions of stars, and if that weren't enough, He created billions of other galaxies across the universe. When finished, in verse 18, He observed that all these created heavenly bodies were "good."

The sixth and final time God makes this observation is on day six after having created human beings. Creation was now complete. God enjoyed seeing how His carefully designed planet was now full of plant, animal, and human life, and how each kind of life was beneficial to the others. His planet was no longer "formless, empty, and dark" as it was at the beginning (verse 2). He had created a living paradise. His conclusion in verse 31 was that it was not just "good," but "very good." He was right! The weather, instead of being extreme and causing death and destruction as it does today through floods, droughts, tornadoes, and hurricanes, was perfect all the time. The planet, rather than being in upheaval and causing chaos as it does today through earthquakes, tsunamis, and volcanoes, was the ideal place for plants, animals, and humans to share life. There was no death among animals and humans, as all were vegetarians (verses 29-30). There were no threats between humans and animals, only support and companionship. There was no human on human evil. God had accomplished His creation goal, and everything was "very good."

For those of you who are thinking that today things are not nearly as "good" as described here, you will find a clear explanation in the Interlude, between Chapters 2 and 3.

Now back to our main focus: What did God mean when He looked at His newly created animals and declared them to be "good"? Maybe God's declaration, "It is good," refers to the immense variety of types of animals He created. For example, He designed and created both vertebrates and invertebrates. Vertebrates are animals which have internal skeletons, including a backbone and a spinal cord. He made many kinds of vertebrates, such as mammals, birds, fish, amphibians, and reptiles, with a great variety of animals within each of these five categories.

God made even more invertebrates than vertebrates. Instead of a backbone, invertebrates have an exoskeleton, that is, an external skeleton such as a shell. God made numerous kinds of invertebrates, but the largest group is the arthropods. They lay eggs and have jointed feet, segmented bodies, and exoskeletons. Arthropods include insects such as grasshoppers, beetles, butterflies, dragonflies, and ants; arachnids or spiders; crustaceans such as shrimp, crabs, lobsters, and crawdads; and millipedes and centipedes. The invertebrates also include a great variety of mollusks, such as oysters, clams, snails, squid, and octopuses. A wide variety of cnidarians, including jellyfish, coral, and sea anemones, belong to the group of invertebrates. The Creator also designed the spiny-skinned echinoderms, which include the starfish, sea urchins, and sand dollars. To top off invertebrate variety, He made sponges and worms. God saw this huge variety and felt that it was "good"! He was right!

Perhaps God's acknowledgement, "It is good," refers to the beauty God built into His animals. Animals are beautiful when they demonstrate their athletic skills of running, swimming, or flying at high speeds. Some jump high off the ground or out of the water, and others demonstrate amazing strength. Animals are also pleasing because of their colors. The colors of the Macau, peacock, hummingbird, butterfly, beetle, and many fish we see while snorkeling dazzle our eyes! Animals are beautiful in the playfulness they show us and in the affection they so generously give us. Yes, the beauty of God's created animals was and is truly "good"!

God's announcement, "It is good," might refer to the purposes the animals would fulfill. They were going to entertain us humans at zoos, aquatic parks, safari parks, rodeos, and circuses. We are thrilled when we can swim with dolphins or walk with lions. Animals entertain us in movies and documentaries. Even more important than entertainment, animals provide us with a type of companionship that no human can furnish. Furthermore, we now realize that some of God's animals are also skilled at promoting healing in our broken lives. Chapter 4 goes into this in more detail. Yes, the purposes of God's created animals were and are decidedly "good"!

I think that God's "It is good" as applied to the creation of the animals refers to their variety, beauty, and purpose. What do you think? Can you add to the list?

"according to their kinds" (Genesis 1:21, 24, 25)

We know that this phrase is important because it is repeated seven times during the creation of the animals. It gives us great insight into how God created the animal kingdom. As we will see, it helps us understand the different families of animals which we observe today.

Many creation scientists believe that the Hebrew word for "kind" means approximately what the term "family" means in taxonomical terminology. As an example, let's look at the classification of the tiger. Its kingdom is animal, its phylum is vertebrate, its class is mammal, its order is carnivore, its <u>family</u> is cat (Felidae), its genus is Panthera, and its species is Panthera tigris. God created the cat family or kind, which includes not only tigers, but also lions, bobcats, panthers, and domestic cats. The animals of each family have similar anatomical characteristics and can produce offspring only with another of their own family. Even though members of a family share many of the same characteristics, their DNA also permits great variety, but always within the limits of the family DNA. For example, in the dog family, there is great variation of physical characteristics, but all dogs belong to the same family. The same is true for all animal families, such as the deer, horse, bear, and finch families.

It is helpful to understand that God created the animals according to their kinds or families, because this fits perfectly with the evidence we observe in the world of animals. The imaginary tree of life on which every animal has evolved from another family of animals, and all animals have their origin in just one animal, is not supported by what we observe. We do not see animals from one family slowly evolving into an animal of another family. We already know this can't happen because of the limitations both in the content of the DNA and in the options for breeding. Also, in the world of fossils, we don't see legitimate transitional forms between families. Ancient fossils fit into our current classes of families or kinds.

God did a great job of creating the animals. By creating them "after their kinds," He produced a beautiful animal kingdom in which there is both unity (all cats belong to the cat family) and diversity (so many different types of cats)!

God blessed them and said, "Be fruitful and increase in number." (Genesis 1:22)

Verse 22 reminds us that God blessed the animals and said, "Be fruitful and increase in number and fill the water in the seas, and let the birds increase on the earth." This command is hugely important. It was one miracle to create the great variety of adult animals, but it was equally overwhelming that in most cases He gave each species a male and female version with complementary reproductive systems by which they procreate the life He originally created. God must love the animals. He not only created them, but also made sure they could reproduce generation after generation.

God created many different types of reproductive systems for the animal world. Mammals have external genitalia, which are the penis and the vulva, and the internal organs, the testicles and ovaries, that produce the sperm and egg. The egg is fertilized internally by the sperm, producing a zygote, or the first cell of the offspring. In the case of many fish, the female first lays her eggs in the water and the male passes by with his sperm to fertilize them. Observing some insects, we see that the male deposits the sperm in the female by means of external genitalia. Her reproductive system then permits the sperm to fertilize her eggs, and she expels them for development. Each animal reproductive system created by God represents His incredible biological engineering and profound love of life.

Fun Fact: "Be fruitful and increase in number" also answers the question, "Which came first, the chicken or the egg?" From God's command we know that adult chickens came first. He gave them the miraculous ability to reproduce themselves and commanded them to do so. Mr. and Mrs. Chicken obeyed, acted and Mrs. Chicken started laying fertilized eggs!

Animal Systems

To be in awe of God's created animals by looking at their fascinating bodies from the outside doesn't do justice to their eye-popping complexity. What is on the inside of animals is even more impressive! Like humans, most animals have about 12 body systems. We just looked at one of them, the reproductive system.

Animals must have a respiratory system in order to extract oxygen from their environment and expel carbon dioxide. This respiratory system is complex in each animal, though the make-up of these systems varies: lungs in mammals, gills in fish, and spiracles in many insects.

Animals need a circulatory system in order to transport oxygen to every cell in their bodies. God gave vertebrates a circulatory system, powered by the heart, which consists of arteries, veins, and capillaries carrying oxygen-rich blood. Invertebrates have a simpler yet awesomely designed system. In every animal, the respiratory and circulatory systems must work hand in hand. One cannot function without the other.

The digestive system is essential to break down the food which fuels their metabolism. God created a wide variety of animal digestive systems. The vertebrate system usually includes a mouth, throat, stomach, intestines, and anus, along with organs such as the liver and kidneys, and the all-important digestive enzymes. These digestive systems, whether in a grasshopper or in an elephant, are masterpieces of design!

Animals must have a nervous system in order to send, receive and process nerve and sensory impulses, and to coordinate muscle movement. The vertebrate system consists of three components: the central, peripheral, and autonomic subsystems. The complexity of the animal nervous systems is astonishing!

The <u>integumentary</u> system is required in order to protect animals from the hazards of their environment and regulate their body temperature. God created a wide variety of integumentary systems, which include the shells of clams, the feathers of birds, the scales of fish, and the hair of mammals. Other components include skin, claws, nails, and hooves.

A <u>skeletal</u> system is also a necessity, though God made a wide variety of these. Insects and crustaceans have a hard, external body covering made of chitin. Sharks and rays are held together by cartilage, and vertebrate bones are made mostly of calcium. In most cases, functioning hand in hand with the skeletal system is the <u>muscular</u> system to allow the animal both to move and control its movements. Vertebrates also have an <u>endocrine</u> system (glands and hormones) in order to keep body functions fine-tuned, a <u>lymphatic</u> system (nodes and lymph) to provide plasma to the blood, and an <u>immune</u> system which identifies and destroys enemy pathogens.

In reality, this brief introduction to the animals' body systems and their functions doesn't do justice to the profound intricacy of each system. Here we are only scratching the surface, but it does help us stand in awe of the animal world.

When we talk about a system, like the brake system in our cars, we know right away that someone had to design and create it. Systems, especially biological ones, don't come into being on their own, or by accident, or through an unguided process. The complexity of animal body systems which permit them to live, grow, survive, and procreate, not only increases our admiration for the animals themselves, but also for the One who designed and created them.

Animal Cells

Reviewing the elaborate body systems of animals inspires applause. Even more exciting is to stop and think how all the organs which make up the functioning parts of these body systems are made of cells. Insects are probably made of millions of cells, small animals of billions, and large animals of trillions! Though God made numerous kinds of cells which all fulfill distinct functions, every cell is a microcosm of life itself.

A cell of an organism is the smallest structural unit capable of functioning on its own. Every cell in every animal has a variety of specialized parts called organelles. Each organelle performs a vital function. Here are a few examples: The <u>cell membrane</u> executes a skin-like function in the cell. It surrounds and protects the cell and recognizes other nearby cells. It is semipermeable, permitting acceptable substances to pass through. Filling the membrane is the <u>cytoplasm</u>, a semi-fluid solution which permits the other parts of the cell to move around freely inside the cell. The <u>nucleus</u> serves a brain-like function and contains the genetic code for producing new cells. The <u>Golgi apparatus</u> receives proteins, processes them, sorts them and then sends them to their destination. The <u>mitochondria</u> are the power stations of the cell, breaking down food and producing energy. The <u>vacuoles</u> operate as warehouses, where both food and waste products are stored. The complexity and functionality of cells point not to a random process, but to a master Designer Creator.

Every part of every animal is made up of these hugely complex cells. In a dog, millions of cells bond together to make a strand of hair, a tooth, part of the tongue or nose, the blood vessels, the liver, the stomach lining, the paws and so on. It's fun to go behind the scenes of the creation of animals to capture more completely the huge miracle which God enacted on days five and six.

Animal DNA

Animal body systems are elaborate, and the cells of which they are made are even more so. But there's nothing quite like the DNA molecule in the nucleus of each animal cell to make us stand in awe! Animal bodies need replacement cells all the time, and DNA makes this possible. Cells are made of proteins and other chemicals, and proteins are made of amino acids, also known as the building blocks of life. DNA tells the amino acids how to bond together to make the right protein to make the correct cell. The making of each replacement cell depends on the work of DNA!

When it comes to making new babies, the DNA molecule contains the complete genetic code. Let's take the example of the giraffe. When the male and female sex cells unite, the first new cell gets half its chromosomes, containing the DNA, from its father and half from its mother. In the DNA of that first cell is found the complete genetic code of the baby. In other words, the DNA contains all the information which will guide the growth of the baby giraffe in its mother's womb. From conception, the blueprint for the construction of the baby's heart, liver, eyes, skin, hooves, brain, bones, and muscles is all encoded in the DNA.

The DNA is the blueprint for the new baby, and also the construction company. In perfect timing, the DNA will build the millions of brain cells, bone cells, skin cells, blood cells, hair cells, vein and artery cells, etc., until the baby is a complete giraffe, waiting to be born. As it builds each new cell, the DNA also has a system of reviewing each one to make sure it is exactly as it should be.

Not only is the DNA the blueprint and the construction company for the new offspring, it is also the transportation company. It makes sure each new cell is transported to where it needs to go. We wouldn't want a bone cell to be taken to form part of the heart muscle, or a hoof cell transported to form part of the brain! When God told the animals to "be fruitful and increase in number," they didn't have to worry about how to make this happen. Having created their reproductive systems and DNA, God himself put procreation in gear.

Now we can start to understand why each DNA molecule has so much intricate information in it, enough to fill many books! When we think about sophisticated information in general, we know that it had to come from an intelligent mind. The same is true of the detailed network of information in the DNA molecule. It could not have come into existence by accident or through some random process. It had to come from an ingenious mind. It came from the mind of the God who created it. For Him who is all-knowing and all-powerful, it was easy. The abundant and complex information in the DNA molecule is a strong testimony that the animal kingdom was created by a brilliant Designer.

Have you enjoyed going behind the scenes of the creation of the animals? We have done this first by looking at "It is good," "according to their kinds," and "Be fruitful and increase in number." We also took time to think about animal systems, cells and DNA. Each of these mini studies confirms that in their creation God was showing great love for the animals. He truly is *The Greatest Animal Lover*!

CHAPTER 2

PROVISION

We often think about how God provides for the needs of us humans but seldom think about how He provides for the needs of animals. But we should, because He does. Jesus talked about this on multiple occasions. Once, when teaching His disciples not to worry, He spoke of God's care for the birds.

> *Look at the birds of the air; they do not sow or reap or store away in barns, and yet your heavenly Father feeds them. Are you not much more valuable than they? (Matthew 6:26)*

Jesus meant that God is actively involved in providing for the needs of birds, and by implication, of all animals. This is also a common idea in the Old Testament. One example is Psalm 147:9.

> *He provides food for the cattle and for the young ravens when they call.*

Actually, God has been intimately involved in providing for the needs of animals since the days of Creation. He does this because He loves them!

In this chapter we will explore how God provides for His animals first through His creation of Earth and then through His command that humans be their caretakers. We will see once again that He is *The Greatest Animal Lover.*

1. Genesis 1:1-19 – God Provides a Perfect Home

God created Planet Earth not only as a home for humans, but also for the sake of animals. Isaiah 45:18 probably refers to both humans and animals.

> *For this is what the Lord says – he who created the heavens, he is God; he who fashioned and made the earth, he founded it; he did not create it to be empty but formed it to be inhabited – he says: "I am the Lord, and there is no other."*

It's no wonder that of the six days of Creation, only the last two were dedicated to the creation of animal and human life. The first four days of Creation were used by God to prepare an ideal living space for humans and every kind of animal. Let's take a day by day look at how God was providing for the animal kingdom through the creation of this planet and beyond.

Day One, verses 3-5

¹ In the beginning God created the heavens and the earth. ² Now the earth was formless and empty, darkness was over the surface of the deep, and the Spirit of God was hovering over the waters.³ And God said, "Let there be light," and there was light. ⁴

God saw that the light was good, and he separated the light from the darkness. ⁵ God called the light "day," and the darkness he called "night." And there was evening, and there was morning— the first day.

According to the Bible, this is how our planet began, not by some unexplainable explosion, but by the loving, creative acts of an all-powerful God. Verse 1 says that at the beginning of day one God "created the heavens and the earth." We understand this to mean that at this moment God was creating the raw material out of which He would form Planet Earth and the universe. Verse 2 explains this: "Now the earth was formless and empty, darkness was over the surface of the deep." God was just warming up. For six days, He would be giving order to that which was "formless," filling with life that which was "empty," and shedding light on the "darkness."

Right away on day one God takes care of the darkness issue. You can't have life on a planet with no light. Verses 3 and 4 say,

> And God said, "Let there be light," and there was
> light. God saw that the light was good.

God himself supplied this light until day four when He created the solar system with our sun as the new source of light for our planet. We don't know exactly how He provided this temporary light source, but we do know that as the all-powerful Creator-God, it was easy for him. He does not depend on stars to produce light.

Light is necessary for the maintenance of advanced life. Without it, photosynthesis in the plant kingdom could not take place and that would be sad for animals. There would be insufficient oxygen to breathe and no plants for herbivores to eat. But since God created light, animals of all kinds are able to live happily on this planet.

On day one we also see the Creator-God starting to put order into our planet. Verses 4 and 5 say,

> and he separated the light from the darkness. God
> called the light "day" and the darkness he called

"night." And there was evening, and there was morning – the first day.

Here we understand that the light was separated from the darkness, resulting in night and day. I believe this means that the earth was already rotating on its axis, while God's temporary light source was shining on it. God designed the speed of the rotation perfectly for life on the planet – one rotation every 24 hours. If the earth's rotation were slower, daytime would get too hot and nighttime too cold. If it were faster, it would cause ongoing violent weather. God also calibrated the tilt of the earth on its axis at precisely 23.5 degrees. If the earth's tilt were greater, summers would be too hot for life and winters too cold. If the tilt were less, the equator would be too hot and the poles too cold. That both the speed of Earth's rotation and the degree of its axial tilt are fine-tuned for life could hardly have come about by chance. The logical conclusion is that there must be a Master Designer behind it all.

I like to think that when God made sure our planet would enjoy both daytime and nighttime, He was thinking of the nocturnal animals. He was preparing a planet that would be perfect for aardvarks, foxes, owls, bats, bobcats, raccoons and many more. Psalm 104:19-22 mentions this truth.

> [19]*The moon marks off the seasons, and the sun knows when to go down.* [20] *You bring darkness, it becomes night, and all the beasts of the forest prowl.* [21]*The lions roar for their prey and seek their food from God.* [22]*The sun rises, and they steal away; they return and lie down in their dens.*

So right from day one, with the creation of light, daytime and nighttime, and a planet spinning at just the right speed and tilted at just the right angle, we can see God's matchless love not only for humans, but also for His soon to be created animals.

Day Two, verses 6-8

⁶ And God said, "Let there be an expanse between the waters to separate water from water." ⁷ So God made the expanse and separated the water under the expanse from the water above it. And it was so. ⁸ God called the expanse "sky." And there was evening, and there was morning—the second day.

On day two we understand that God was creating an atmosphere for Planet Earth. It wasn't just any haphazard atmosphere, but one which until today has not been discovered on any other planet in the universe. It consists of an expanse of air which was and is perfect for supporting life of all kinds.

The ingenious atmosphere which God created consists of a series of layers. The troposphere goes from sea level up to about six miles. Then comes the stratosphere which stretches from about six to thirty-one miles. Beyond this is the mesosphere from about 31 to 53 miles. And way up there is the thermosphere, followed by the exosphere which is the transition into outer space. Each layer of our atmosphere has its own traits and plays a key role in making Earth the unique, life-supporting planet that it is.

The air of Earth's lower atmosphere has the ideal composition for life. The combination of 21% oxygen, 78% nitrogen, and 1% trace materials is finely tuned for plants, animals and humans. Less oxygen and our dog, cat, or horse would need to use an oxygen mask. More oxygen and forest fires would burn out of control. Both oxygen and nitrogen are the right kinds of gases which permit excess heat to escape from the lower atmosphere. If not for them, our planet would be way too hot for animals and humans.

One of my favorite characteristics of the air of our lower atmosphere is that it is a great environment in which to fly. Air has mass, weight, and pressure, and when you put them together it is a perfect place for lady bugs, dragon flies, bats, hummingbirds, geese, and hawks to enjoy flight. Certainly, God was thinking of His flying animals already on day two when He made our atmosphere.

Day Three, verses 9-13

⁹ And God said, "Let the water under the sky be gathered to one place, and let dry ground appear." And it was so. ¹⁰ God called the dry ground "land," and the gathered waters he called "seas." And God saw that it was good.

¹¹ Then God said, "Let the land produce vegetation: seed-bearing plants and trees on the land that bear fruit with seed in it, according to their various kinds." And it was so. ¹² The land produced vegetation: plants bearing seed according to their kinds and trees bearing fruit with seed in it according to their kinds. And God saw that it was good. ¹³ And there was evening, and there was morning—the third day.

Before day three of Creation, our planet was just mud - water mixed with dirt. But now God would bring form and order to the mud, separating the water from the dirt.

Dry Ground

On this day God created the dry ground and called it land. Geologists help us understand part of God's design for the deep dry ground. They observe that God created three layers: the crust, the mantle, and the core. The crust is the upper layer which goes down about 35 miles. It has a thin layer of soil on top and then a thick layer of bedrock underneath. The middle layer is called the mantle, which is about 1,800 miles thick with temperatures of around 5,000 degrees F. It is from the mantle that volcanos cough up magma, or molten rock. The third or deepest layer is the core, which is divided into the outer and inner cores. The total depth of the earth is about 4,000 miles. It's fun to keep learning more about this dry ground that God created on day three. One thing is sure: He designed it all to be an excellent planet for life.

On the surface of the planet, God created many kinds of terrain, each one forming a habitat for numerous animals. He created mountains (mountain goats), valleys (deer), plains (zebras), deserts (tortoises), forests (bears), and jungles (apes), each with their corresponding weather conditions. Just think about how on days five and six God would create a wide variety of animals which would enjoy life in each of the dry land habitats He created on day three.

It's fascinating to stop and think about all the details God incorporated into the dry land. We wonder at all the kinds of rocks, metals, minerals, and nutrients we find there. Did you know that plants need about 15 different nutrients to remain healthy and productive? Some of these are nitrogen, phosphorus, potassium, calcium, magnesium, and sulfur. Since God created all these nutrients and put them into the soil of our planet on day three of Creation, plants can find all the nutrition they need. How convenient that He also created the roots of plants so that they would be able to extract these life-supporting nutrients from the soil! Remember, whenever plants are blessed, so are the animals which depend on them.

Water

As God separated the dry land from the water, He created the life-giving gift of liquid water. He was generous with water, as 70% of Earth's surface is covered with it, providing habitats for the aquatic animals. He created the salty oceans with their seas and gulfs (dolphins). He placed fresh water in lakes (largemouth bass) at the surface and aquifers below it. He created a vast network of rivers and streams (beavers) across the dry land. He included marshlands and everglades (crocodiles). Each of these types of watery habitats were created for the vast array of animals suited to live in them.

What a great idea God had when He created the water molecule! Full of oxygen, liquid water is the correct place to live if your respiratory system is fashioned to extract oxygen from water. If water freezes, it floats, so the ice doesn't sink and crush all aquatic life. Plus, ice becomes another great habitat for animals such as polar bears and penguins. If that weren't enough, water can also evaporate, become water vapor, be transported by the wind, condense and fall as rain where it is needed on dry land. This hydrological system is one of the Creator's most brilliant ideas for the sustenance of life. The water molecule must come from a Designer and not from a thoughtless process.

Vegetation

Day three was not nearly over when God finished creating the dry land and the bodies of liquid water. The Master Designer continued by creating the first level of life, vegetation (verses 11, 12). At this point God created the first cells along with their DNA. Plants and trees are a key ingredient for animal and human life on Planet Earth. As plants make their food, they give off oxygen, which is a life-sustaining ingredient for animals and humans. At the same time, animals and humans give off carbon dioxide, needed by plants to make their food. It is difficult to imagine that this vital complementariness would come about through an accidental, arbitrary process. Many would conclude that a loving Designer is behind it.

Animals and humans depend on plants for food. The leaves of plants are complex chemical factories which turn nutrients from the ground and energy from the sun into a huge variety of foods. Grazing animals eat grass, and pandas need bamboo. Monkeys love bananas, goats and giraffes enjoy leaves, and fruit bats chew on fruits such as figs and mangos. This is all part of God's original plan. Notice what He says in Genesis 1:30 after having created all the animals:

> *And to all the beasts of the earth and all the birds of the air and all the creatures that move on the ground – everything that has the breath of life in it – I give every green plant for food. And it was so.*

From this we learn that at the beginning of creation all animals were herbivores. There was no death in the animal and human realms. The predator/prey dynamic would only come about when Adam and Eve fell into sin, which will be explained in the Interlude.

I like how Psalm 104:14 reflects on the way God provides for the animals through His creation of vegetation on day three.

> *He makes grass grow for the cattle, and plants for*
> *man to cultivate – bringing forth food from the earth.*

The world of vegetation does more for animals than supply food. Trees are a special blessing to many animals, providing a place to live. Think of all the kinds of birds that make their nests in the trees of their habitat and all the apes and monkeys that live in and swing through trees. Think about how beavers love to use fallen trees to make their houses in streams. How sad life would be for woodpeckers if not for trees! Psalm 104:16-17a expresses this reality.

> *The trees of the Lord are well watered, the cedars of*
> *Lebanon that he planted. There the birds make their*
> *nests.*

Wow! Day three is full of evidence of God providing for the needs of animals through His creative acts.

Day Four, verses 14-19

[14] And God said, "Let there be lights in the expanse of the sky to separate the day from the night, and let them serve as signs to mark seasons, and days and years, [15] and let them be lights in the expanse of the sky to give light on the earth." And it was so. [16] God made two great lights—the greater light to govern the day and the lesser light to govern the night. He also made the stars. [17] God set them in the expanse of the sky to give light on the earth, [18] to govern the day and the night, and to separate light from darkness.

And God saw that it was good. [19] And there was evening, and there was morning—the fourth day.

Day four of Creation was magnificent because on this day God built a solar system for Planet Earth, a galaxy for our solar system, and billions of galaxies to complete the universe. What a Creator! He does love to create little things, like subatomic particles and proteins, but this Master of the nanoworld is also the Master of the macroworld, as we see on day four. The hugeness of the universe and its heavenly bodies never stops blowing our minds. The hypergiant star UY Scuti has a radius approximately 1,700 times that of our sun,[24] and the distance across the universe is measured in billions of light years. God delights in big!

When God created and put in order our solar system, galaxy and universe, He was obviously preparing Earth in many ways to be a splendid place for life of all kinds: plant, animal, and human. Here are just a few examples:

First, He put our solar system at a safe location in the Milky Way galaxy. In other parts of the galaxy, radiation would threaten to snuff out life.

Second, in addition to sister planets, God gave earth the perfect sun. This sun, created on day four, now replaced the temporary light source which God produced for Planet Earth for days one through three. There are trillions of suns in the universe, but very few like ours. It provides enough, but not too much, light, warmth, and energy. It has neither super flares nor super strength coronal mass ejections which would destroy life on Earth. Our sun is uniquely designed to support life on our planet.

Third, within our solar system, God put earth at just the right distance from the sun. Earth is in the habitable zone, where there can be liquid water. If Earth were too close to the sun, the heat would boil the water away, but if too far from the sun, the water would freeze. No liquid water, no advanced life.

Fourth, God gave Earth an elliptical orbit around the sun. We don't get too close or too far away from the warmth, light, and energy of our sun. Due to its nearly circular orbit, Earth is a stable planet, just right for life.

Fifth, He created Earth with just the exact mass for sustaining life. Earth has enough mass so that its gravitational pull holds on to life sustaining gases such as oxygen and nitrogen. If earth's mass were greater, the lighter, poisonous gases would also be retained, and life would cease to exist.

Sixth, God gave Earth a sensational moon which helps sustain life. Our moon's gravitational pull is responsible for the tides and currents in our oceans. If the moon were too large, the ocean's tides would become destructive tsunamis, but if too small, the tides and currents would be insufficient to clean and oxygenate the oceans. That would be sad for all the aquatic animals!

Seventh, He placed a finely tuned magnetic shield around the Earth, which protects living organisms from the harmful radiation of the sun. Without it, all animals and humans would quickly become crispy critters.

These are but a few of the many precisely-tuned parameters which God built into and around Planet Earth. Day four of Creation demonstrates how God was focusing on providing a superb home for living things.

Let's review. On day one God created the raw material for the planet and set it in motion, rotating at just the right speed and angle. In addition, He generated a temporary light source for Earth. On day two God made an awesome atmosphere. On day three He created dry land, watery habitats, and vegetation. On day four God produced Planet Earth's solar system, galaxy, and universe. On each day of Creation and with each new, creative act, God was demonstrating His love for animals by providing them with an ideal place to live.

2. *Genesis 1:26 – God Provides Human Caretakers*

Now we will see that God also provided for His beloved animals by commanding His newly created human beings to care for them. This command is mentioned twice in the creation account. In

Genesis 1:26, as God is getting ready to create man and woman on day six, He says,

> Then God said, "Let us make man in our image, in our likeness, and let them rule over the fish of the sea and the birds of the air, over the livestock, over all the earth, and over all the creatures that move along the ground."

After God created Adam and Eve, He spoke to them the same command in verse 28.

> God blessed them and said to them, "Be fruitful and increase in number; fill the earth and subdue it. Rule over the fish of the sea and the birds of the air and over every living creature that moves on the ground."

Because of this repetition we know that this command was highly important from God's point of view. He was very serious about insisting that the human beings He created be responsible for ruling over or taking care of His animal kingdom. Why? Because animals are an integral part of His global creation and He loves them.

This animal friendly command is repeated in other parts of the Bible. For example, in Psalm 8:6-8 we see that the scope of God's command to humans covers the whole animal kingdom.

> 6You made him ruler over the works of your hands; you put everything under his feet: 7all flocks and herds, and the beasts of the field, 8the birds of the air, and the fish of the sea, all that swim the paths of the seas.

In Genesis 2 there is a heart-warming event which illustrates man's role as caretaker of the animal kingdom. The naming of the animals, each with a male and a female, sets the scene for Adam to notice that he was lacking his life partner. Here is how the naming of the animals is described in Genesis 2:19-20:

> [19]Now the Lord God had formed out of the ground all the beasts of the field and all the birds of the air. He brought them to the man to see what he would name them; and whatever the man called each living creature, that was its name. [20]So the man gave names to all the livestock, the birds of the air and all the beasts of the field.

We learn much from this event. First, it was important to God that the animals have names because He values them. Second, God wanted man to be the name-giver because He wanted humans to have a special bond with and be intimately involved in the world of animals. The naming of the animals was part of man's caretaker role that God had established. Third, God himself brought the animals to Adam for their naming. We don't know exactly how this took place, but perhaps it was like when God would bring the animals to Noah for their entrance into the ark. What we see here is a God who loves animals, and who wants humans to love, respect, and care for them.

This idea of God commanding us to be caretakers of the animal world comes up again in Moses' day. There are many laws given in the Book of Deuteronomy, but when it comes to animals none are more touching than the one in Deuteronomy 22:6-7.

> [6] If you come across a bird's nest beside the road, either in a tree or on the ground, and the mother is sitting on the young or on the eggs, do not take the mother with the young. [7] You may take the young, but be sure to let the mother go, so that it may go well with you and you may have a long life.

Here is a practical application of the general command to rule over the animals. While the eggs or young may be taken for food, the preservation of the species must be respected. God forbids that humans abuse animals by needlessly harming or eliminating them. It's interesting that God is so concerned about His animals that He makes a strong promise to the person who would obey His will for them, "that it may go well with you and you may have a long life." Since God loves animals, He is counting on humans to do a good job of caring for them and showing them all the love and respect that He himself has in His heart for them.

What are some ways that we humans disobey God's command to rule over and take care of the animal world? Here are a few ideas: (1) overfishing the waters, putting in danger the delicate balance of life, (2) damaging or destroying vital animal habitats (land, water or air) for inadequate reasons, (3) needlessly hunting animals for sport or to harvest and sell their body parts, and (4) abusing or mistreating animals which are being raised for food for humans. Can you think of others?

What are some ways that we humans obey God's command to rule over and take care of the animal world? Here are a few ideas: (1) teaching our children, from early on, to be kind and respectful to all animals, (2) learning as much as we can about how to support healthy habitats for animals, (3) learning how to avoid "toxic help" for animals, (4) assuring that zoos, animal parks and circuses do their best to provide a healthy environment and lifestyle for their animals, (5) supporting institutions which do a good job of protecting wildlife from human abuses, and (6) rescuing and adopting abandoned animals. Can you think of others?

In this chapter we have seen that God is indeed *The Greatest Animal Lover.* He demonstrates His love for animals by providing for their needs. He created and sustains a planet which is ideal for their wide variety of habitats, and He commands humans to be their loving and respectful caretakers.

DAMAGED RELATIONSHIPS

The Fact

It is abundantly clear that there exists a tremendous love and respect between humans and animals. It's easy to understand why humans and animals are fond of each other. God designed animals to serve and support humans. We humans love animals because we are created in the image of God, and He is the greatest of all animal lovers.

If you have been thinking that the reality of the relationship between humans and animals is not quite as rosy as described so far in this book, you are correct. Until now, I've painted only half the picture. The other half is not nearly as pretty.

Have you ever been stung by a bee or a wasp? Has a horse ever kicked you, a dog ever bit you, or a cat ever scratched you? Have mosquitoes ruined your picnic, or termites your furniture? Dogs bite and maim. Lions, tigers, bears, and orcas attack and kill their trainers. Elephants trample villagers.

On the night of October 3, 2003, Siegfried and Roy were performing their usual, exciting show which combined magic and big cats.[25] Mantecore, a 380 pound, 7-year-old white tiger, was one of their most trusted cats. He had performed thousands of times with his trainers. Yet that night, for some unknown reason, Mantecore grabbed Roy by the arm and then by the neck. He dragged the performer off-stage behind a curtain. Roy lost most of his blood and was partially paralyzed but has made a remarkable recovery. Mantecore and Roy remained friends until the tiger died 9 years later. Did the tiger mean to harm Roy? We may never know, but the damage was done.

On February 25, 2010, at SeaWorld in Orlando, Dawn Brancheau, an experienced orca trainer, was killed by one of the whales.[26] Tilikum, a 12,000-pound orca whose performing name was Shamu, had spent many years at SeaWorld. He and Brancheau were old buddies. But that day when they were performing together in the water, Tilikum grabbed Brancheau's dry ponytail, and violently pulled her under the water, killing her. We don't know if the violence was on purpose.

When my wife and I were camping and hiking recently in Arizona, Utah and Montana, one of the constant warnings was to beware of the bears. In the summer of 2016, an off-duty park ranger was riding his mountain bike near Glacier National Park.[27] Coming down a hill and around a corner at high speed, he surprised a grizzly. The grizzly knocked him off his bike and mauled him to death. A friend riding with the ranger was able to escape. This was the 10th grizzly-related human death in or near Glacier Park since its opening in 1910.

But animals are not the only ones in this animal/human relationship who can be hurtful. Have you ever seen another person being mean to an animal? We have to teach our little children to be gentle, not harsh, with our pets. Animals are enslaved, starved and mistreated. They are sometimes hunted for invalid reasons, for "sport" or "fun." Humans cause some animals to become extinct.

The Reason

We come back to the same questions. Why are humans capable of mistreating instead of loving animals? Why are animals capable of hurting humans instead of loving and supporting them? The answer to these questions is found in Genesis 3, where we read about the first humans choosing to rebel against their powerful, yet loving, Creator God. Let's take a look.

At the end of Genesis 2, Planet Earth, and everything in it, created by God, was functioning beautifully. All of life, including plants, animals, and humans, was healthy and happy. Love, admiration, servanthood, and kindness dominated the relationship between humans and animals. Though we aren't given details about how humans and animals related to one another before the fall into sin, we can imagine some things. There were no threats of harm, neither of animals toward Adam and Eve, nor of the first humans toward the animals. Can you imagine the elephant inviting Eve to ride on his back? I can. Can you imagine the lion challenging Adam to a wrestling match, just for the fun of it? I can. Can you imagine an eagle, a coyote, a mountain goat, and a tiger joining Adam and Eve for a vegetarian picnic lunch? I can. What other scenes can you imagine took place between humans and animals before the tragic fall into sin?

Planet Earth was the perfect place for plants, animals, and humans. Weather was just the way God originally planned it. There were breezes, but no damaging wind storms, hurricanes, or tornadoes. There was tectonic movement, but no damaging earthquakes or volcanoes. There were no disastrous floods or droughts. With both a perfect planet and perfect weather, life was beautiful every day for plants, animals, and humans.

But the perfection of the planet and of the relationship between humans and animals came to a screeching halt when Adam and Eve disobeyed God. The incomparable God who created animals and humans was not only all-powerful and full of love, He was also moral and just. He had given Adam (and Eve) a warning in Chapter 2.

> *[15]The Lord God took the man and put him in the Garden of Eden to work it and take care of it. [16]And the Lord God commanded the man "You are free to eat from any tree in the garden; [17]But you must not eat from the tree of the knowledge of good and evil, for when you eat of it you will surely die."*

The warning was clear. Adam and Eve had abundant choices of trees from which to eat. There was only one restriction: Don't eat the fruit from the tree of the knowledge of good and evil. When God said, "for when you eat of it you will surely die," He didn't mean that they would literally, physically die on the spot. He meant they would become sinners, and as such, their relationship with their holy Creator God would be broken (spiritual death); their bodies would age and die (physical death); and if not forgiven, they would experience eternity in hell (eternal death).

Sadly, as Genesis 3 begins, Adam and Eve are considering doing exactly what God had warned them not to do! Under the influence of the devil, in the form of one of God's good created animals, the snake, Eve foolishly becomes open to the idea of disobeying God's clear command. She eats of the forbidden fruit of the tree of the knowledge of good and evil, and then invites Adam to join in her rebellion. He also falls into the sin of disobedience by eating the fruit (Genesis 3:1-6).

The disastrous results of this sin become an avalanche of brokenness. First, Adam and Eve now struggle with the ugly feelings of guilt. They sew together fig leaves to cover the shame of their sinfulness (Genesis 3:7). Second, their perfect, peaceful relationship with God is broken. He comes looking for them in the Garden. Before sinning, they would run to meet him, but now they run to hide from Him. Their guilt leads to feelings of fear in God's presence (Genesis 3:8-10). Third, when God confronts them with their sin, they show themselves to be incapable of accepting the responsibility of their actions. Adam blames Eve and God. Eve blames the serpent.

Now the relationship between humans will often be scarred by the attempt to cast the blame on one another (Genesis 3:11-13).

Genesis 3:14-19 shows that the repercussions of Adam and Eve's sin did not only affect the human/human and human/divine relationships. Their whole planet, and everything which lives on it, were negatively affected. The plants, animals, and the planet itself all came under God's judgment, not because they shared in the guilt of sin, but because they were created for Adam and Eve and were to be under man's responsibility.

Verse 14 shows the effects of sin on the animal kingdom.

> [14]So the Lord God said to the serpent, "Because you have done this, cursed are you above all the livestock and all the wild animals! You will crawl on your belly and you will eat dust all the days of your life."

The serpent came under God's punishment, not because it was morally responsible, but because of its role in the fall into sin. The Bible text states that the snake underwent some anatomical changes, but what is important is that to this day, the whole animal kingdom is suffering under God's chastisement upon Adam and Eve's sin. Before the fall, all animals were herbivores. There was no death in the animal and human kingdoms. Animals killing and eating other animals was not God's original, perfect plan. Animals would never have hurt humans before the fall into sin, but now their relationship was flawed. Since the fall into sin, humans and animals are a potential threat to one another instead of a blessing.

Verses 16a and 19b show the ill effects of sin on the human body.

> [16]To the woman he said, "I will greatly increase your pains in childbearing; with pain you will give birth to children."

> [19]. . . until you return to the ground, since from it you were taken; for dust you are and to dust you will return."

The human reproductive system would no longer function perfectly. There would be great pain for the mother as she gives birth, and many details in the reproductive process would go wrong (inability to conceive, miscarriage, erectile disfunction, prenatal diseases, etc.). It was not only the human reproductive system which came under God's sentence; rather, our whole body is subject to malfunction, disease, aging and death.

Verses 17-19 demonstrate that God's just penalty on human sin also affected the plant kingdom and the planet itself.

> [17]To Adam he said, "Because you listened to your wife and ate from the tree about which I commanded you, 'You must not eat of it,' cursed is the ground because of you; through painful toil you will eat of it all the days of your life. [18]It will produce thorns and thistles for you, and you will eat the plants of the field. [19]By the sweat of your brow you will eat your food until you return to the ground, since from it you were taken; for dust you are and to dust you will return."

The plant world would now be capable of being a curse in addition to a blessing. There would be thorns, thistles, and other weeds which interfere in the harvest. Man would still farm and eat from the plants, but now agricultural work would be filled with challenges. Diseases, fungi, and rodents would attack our plants and crops. Farming for food would no longer be easy-peasy, but hard work.

Thorns and thistles were only a small part of how the planet would suffer because of God's retribution for man's sin. The planet's previously perfect weather would become a threat to plants, animals, and humans. Floods, droughts, hurricanes, tornadoes, and other kinds of severe storms would threaten man's possessions and well-being. The planet's tectonic movements would become a threat to man's safety, with earthquakes and volcanoes wreaking havoc on plant, animal, and human life. Planet Earth, though still demonstrating much of the beauty, order, and provision with which God created it, was now broken and under God's judgment because of man's sin.

Hope of Restoration

St. Paul described this extensive sin-produced malfunction in the created world in Romans 8:18-23.

> [18]*I consider that our present sufferings are not worth comparing with the glory that will be revealed in us.* [19]*The creation waits in eager expectation for the sons of God to be revealed.* [20]*For the creation was subjected to frustration, not by its own choice, but by the will of the one who subjected it, in hope* [21]*that the creation itself will be liberated from its bondage to decay and brought into the glorious freedom of the children of God.* [22]*We know that the whole creation has been groaning as in the pains of childbirth right up to the present time.* [23]*Not only so, but we ourselves, who have the first-fruits of the Spirit, groan inwardly as we wait eagerly for our adoption as sons, the redemption of our bodies.*

Let's look at this passage verse by verse.

> [18]*I consider that our present sufferings are not worth comparing with the glory that will be revealed in us.*

Since the fall into sin, human life is plagued with illness, aging, natural disasters, accidents, hatred, injustice, violence, and war. But what we suffer in this broken world does not compare with the life of peace and satisfaction which we will enjoy at the end of time in the new heaven and new earth.

*¹⁹The creation waits in eager expectation for the sons
of God to be revealed.*

The "creation" that waits here refers to all of creation except human beings. Included would be the planet itself along with the plant and animal kingdoms. Paul is personifying these things, as if they were aware of their brokenness and eagerly waiting for their renewal on the Last Day. The phrase "for the sons of God to be revealed" refers to the Last Day, when Jesus returns, raises the dead, restores all of creation, and inaugurates the final stage of eternal life in the new heaven and new earth for all those who believed in Him.

*²⁰For the creation was subjected to frustration, not by its
own choice, but by the will of the one who subjected it,*

The created world (the planet and the plant and animal kingdoms) is currently frustrated. St. Paul again personifies them, speaking of their frustration due to their brokenness. They hurt humans but they know they weren't created for that purpose. God created the weather to be a blessing to humans, but its irritation is that its floods, droughts, and storms cause harm. The planet was created to be a pure blessing to humans, but its dissatisfaction is that its earthquakes and volcanoes cause pain and destruction, not blessing. The sun is frustrated because it causes sunburns when it was created only to bring warmth and light to humans. Vegetation is disgruntled when thorns rip through skin and weeds damage crops. Animals are disheartened when they bite, maul, sting or do any kind of damage to humans. They know that they were created by God to support their human companions.

This agonizing frustration of all parts of the created world is not their fault. They have been subjected to this situation because of man's sin and God's just reaction to it. When Adam and Eve sinned, God's sentence didn't fall only on them, but on the planet, plants, and animals for which they were supposed to be caretakers.

in hope [21]that the creation itself will be liberated from
its bondage to decay and brought into the glorious
freedom of the children of God.

There is hope for this frustrated planet with its plant and animal kingdoms. All of creation, which is broken right now, is "eagerly waiting" (verse 19) and "hoping" (verse 20) for the day when it will be liberated from the frustration of causing harm to humans, which is part of its "bondage to decay." That will be the day when God's judgment on human sin will be ended and the curse lifted, and creation will get back to functioning as it was before the fall into sin. This restoration, for which the created world waits and hopes, will occur when "the children of God enter their glorious freedom" on the Last Day when Jesus returns. Not only will we believers receive resurrection bodies, but all of creation will be restored. Sin and its effects will be gone, and creation will be liberated from its frustration and decay. All of creation will be a pure blessing to humans, just as it was before the fall into sin. Our resurrected bodies and the new heaven and new earth will be a perfect match.

This complete restoration was foretold in Genesis 3, right in the middle of all the judgments mentioned earlier. God promised that the future Messiah would "crush" the devil's plan to destroy God's beloved creation (Genesis 3:15). This promise was fulfilled in Jesus' suffering, death, and resurrection, when He received all of God's punishment on our sin in our place. Jesus' saving ministry not only redeemed humans but made possible the renewal of all creation!

[22]*We know that the whole creation has been groaning*
as in the pains of childbirth right up to the present time.

St. Paul here continues giving the created world a personality. Not only is creation's current situation annoying, it is downright painful! But in the midst of this pain and frustration of being hurtful to humans, creation maintains the hope of being liberated from its irritation and torment.

> *23No only so, but we ourselves, who have the first-fruits*
> *of the Spirit, groan inwardly as we wait eagerly for our*
> *adoption as sons, the redemption of our bodies.*

We believers in Jesus, like the planet, the universe, and the plant and animal kingdoms, are also eagerly waiting for that great day of restoration. We have "the first-fruits of the Spirit," that is, the blessings of forgiveness, peace, and purpose which we received upon believing in Jesus as our Savior. But our salvation will not be complete until Jesus returns, and we start our new lives in the new heaven and new earth. "Our adoption as sons" refers to our initiation in the new heaven and new earth, while "the redemption of our bodies" points to the resurrection of the dead which will occur in the same time frame. Then we believers and all of creation will have the privilege of living in that sin-free world for eternity! No more hatred, war, pain, illness, or death. No more sorrow and tears. No more natural disasters, thorns, or thistles. No more animals hurting humans nor humans hurting animals. We will be back to life the way God planned it in the first place!

Conclusion

While it's true that humans and animals love and admire each other, our relationship is damaged. We are capable of hurting each other, and we do. But the reason for this is no mystery. The imperfection in the human/animal relationship is part of the disfunction we observe all around us. It is the result of human sin and God's judgment on it. The encouraging truth is that because of Jesus we have the hope of seeing all this brokenness restored to wholeness at the end of the world in the new heaven and new earth.

CHAPTER 3

RESCUE

After the fall into sin, and God's harsh sentence on plants, animals, humans, and the planet itself, you would think that humans would have responded to God's judgment by seeking to do His will. But that's not what happened. Human behavior went from bad to worse. Look at this description from Genesis 6:5-6, 11:

> *⁵The Lord saw how great man's wickedness on the earth had become, and that every inclination of the thoughts of his heart was only evil all the time. ⁶The Lord was grieved that he had made man on the earth, and his heart was filled with pain.*
>
> *¹¹Now the earth was corrupt in God's sight and was full of violence.*

Isn't it sad that this wonderful God's heart was filled with pain because of the evil behavior of His created humans? We don't know if human wickedness in the time before the flood was worse than it is now. We do know that sin and violence had become pervasive. Because of His great love for His created world, God was so grieved by man's sin that He was sorry He had created mankind in the first place!

Just as God's initial punishment on Adam and Eve's sin was strong, so was His follow-up judgment on man's growing affection for sin and violence. God became so fed up with human sin in the days of Noah that He decided to wipe out humanity along with its exaggerated sinfulness. God's upcoming chastisement on human sin is described in Genesis 6:7, 12-13.

> *7So the Lord said, "I will wipe mankind, whom I have created, from the face of the earth; men and animals, and creatures that move along the ground, and birds of the air; for I am grieved that I have made them."*

> *12God saw how corrupt the earth had become, for all the people on earth had corrupted their ways. 13So God said to Noah, "I am going to put an end to all people, for the earth is filled with violence because of them. I am surely going to destroy both them and the earth."*

What a big deal human sin is in God's eyes! We tend to make light of it, but for a holy and just God, sin cannot be tolerated. It must be punished, and the punishment is death, temporal and eternal. What would God's just reaction be to man's rebellion? The answer comes through clearly in Genesis 6:17.

> *17I am going to bring floodwaters on the earth to destroy all life under the heavens, every creature that has the breath of life in it. Everything on earth will perish.*

God would initiate a world-wide flood through which all land and air-based life would die. God would push the re-start button on His created world by washing away the terrible sinfulness that filled it. How heavy it made God's heart when He had to destroy the plant, animal, and human life which He had so lovingly created!

God's justice responded to human sin in a drastic and effective way, but in His love and mercy, He made sure of two things. First, even though almost all humans would die, the human race would be saved. Second, even though almost all animals would die, His beloved animal kingdom would also be saved from the waters of the flood. God couldn't imagine a Planet Earth without them! He rescued humans and animals through a man named Noah and his great big boat. Let's look at five key components of the Great Flood: (1) Noah, (2) the ark, (3) the floodwaters, (4) the animals, and (5) the God of the flood.

Noah

We know quite a bit about Noah. He lived after the fall into sin and before the Great Flood, probably about the year 2,350 BC. In those days, God granted humans longer lives to ensure the expansion of the human race. Noah lived to be 950 years old (Genesis 9:28-29). His father, Lamech, lived to be 777 years old, and his grandpa, Methuselah, lived longer than any known human, 969 years!

It appears that Noah was a farmer. When he was born, his dad named him Noah, which means "comfort," and said, "He will comfort us in the labor and painful toil of our hands caused by the ground the Lord has cursed" (Genesis 5:29). Lamech pre-planned for little Noah to be an expert farmer, and this was confirmed after the flood when Noah is described as "a man of the soil," who "proceeded to plant a vineyard" (Genesis 9:20). This agricultural background certainly came in handy as Noah worked with the animals God sent to him and raised and stored the food for the year-long journey.

Noah was dedicated to living for God's glory. This was important to God, because most of the people in Noah's day were living in open sin and violence. Genesis 6:8-9 says,

"But Noah found favor in the eyes of the Lord. . . Noah was a righteous man, blameless among the people of his time, and he walked with God."

What a tribute! Noah didn't just love the Lord; he tried to live a life which would be pleasing to His Creator God. After the flood the first thing Noah did was build an altar of thankfulness to God for His salvation from the flood (Genesis 8:20). God decided that this obedient Noah would be His man for rescuing humans and animals from annihilation in the coming deluge.

Noah was a good listener and very obedient. Genesis 6:22 and 7:5 say,

"Noah did everything just as God commanded him."
"And Noah did all that the Lord commanded him."

Several times while building the ark, calling the animals, and disembarking after the flood, we see Noah doing everything exactly as the Lord had instructed him. Listening and obeying were both important traits that God saw in Noah.

Finally, we know that during the years of the ark's construction, Noah tried to share the truth of God with the people around him. Look at II Peter 2:5:

"If (God) did not spare the ancient world when he brought the flood on its ungodly people, but protected Noah, a preacher of righteousness, and seven others. . ."

While Noah was busy building, he preached both God's judgment on sin and God's mercy in offering forgiveness to sinners. It appears he had a tough audience in those days.

What about those ship-building skills? When, where, and how did Noah obtain this ability? We don't know! We do know that under God's guidance, and by God's grace, he built a huge ship which withstood the rigors of the flood and provided safety for eight humans and thousands of animals!

The Ark

The ark which Noah built under God's instruction was colossal! Here are the exact directives given by God to Noah in Genesis 6:14-16:

> [14]So make yourself an ark of cypress wood; make rooms in it and coat it with pitch inside and out. [15]This is how you are to build it: the ark is to be 450 feet long, 75 feet wide and 45 feet high. [16]Make a roof for it and finish the ark to within 18 inches of the top. Put a door in the side of the ark and make lower, middle and upper decks.

The ark was designed by God to fulfill various purposes. First, it had to be strong and proportional enough to withstand the torrential storm of the flood. It didn't have to be navigable and needed no sails, rudder, or even a steering wheel. All it had to do was float and survive the floodwaters. Second, it had to be large and versatile enough to house Noah's family of eight, plus thousands of animals, and all the food, water, and veterinarian supplies for a one-year voyage. For God, who fashioned and created the whole universe, designing this boat was effortless.

How long did it take to build this huge ship? We don't know exactly. We do know that when Noah was first introduced in Chapter 5:32, he was 500 years old, and he and Mrs. Noah were starting their family. We also know that Noah was 600 years old when he and his family and the animals entered the ark at the beginning of the flood (Genesis 7:6-7); therefore, we can assume it took less than 100 years to build the ark. Even employing workers from the community, this much time would be needed to build such a large vessel.

In Hebron, Kentucky, just south of Cincinnati, Ohio, stands a full-sized replica of Noah's ark, completed in 2016, by an institution called Answers in Genesis.[28] The public is welcome to visit the Ark Encounter.[29] My wife and I visited the site to help prepare for this chapter. Over a football field and a half long, the structure is incredible. We walked through the three levels and learned how Noah and his family may have placed the cages and stalls for the different sized animals. We learned how Noah may have dealt with ventilation and lighting issues, food and water storage challenges, and waste removal. Thought was also given to how these eight people may have divided the labor of feeding and cleaning up after so many animals. By the way, if you would have been one of the thousands of animals on board this boat designed by God and built by Noah, you would not have felt cramped. Whether you were a pigeon or a T-Rex, space was plentiful!

The Floodwaters

As we focus on how God saved not only humans but also animals from the disastrous effects of the flood, it is important that we understand the extent of this deluge. Some people mistakenly think that Genesis is speaking of a large, local flood, but this is not correct. We know that it was a world-wide flood, first because of the description of who and what died in the floodwaters. Genesis 7:21-23 says,

> [21]*Every living thing that moved on the earth perished, birds, livestock, wild animals, all the creatures that swarm over the earth, and all mankind.* [22]*Everything on dry land that had the breath of life in its nostrils died.* [23]*Every living thing on the face of the earth was wiped out; men and animals and the creatures that move along the ground and the birds of the air were wiped from the earth. Only Noah was left, and those with him in the ark.*

The repetition of "every" and "everything" indicates that literally all land animals and birds died in the flood, along with all humans on the planet. The focus is not what died in a local area of the earth, but on the whole "face of the earth," thus describing a world-wide flood.

We also know the flood covered the whole planet because of the description of what was covered by the waters. Look at Genesis 7:18-20:

> [18]*The waters rose and increased greatly on the earth, and the ark floated on the surface of the water. [19]They rose greatly on the earth, and all the high mountains under the entire heavens were covered. [20]The waters rose and covered the mountains to a depth of more than twenty feet.*

The flood waters didn't just cover a region of the planet; they covered the whole planet. This is emphasized in verse 19, "all the high mountains under the entire heavens were covered."

According to the Bible, there is no doubt that this was a world-wide flood. But the next question is legitimate. Is there enough water on the planet to accomplish this? According to Genesis 7:11-12, there is plenty of water.

> [11]*On that day all the springs of the great deep burst forth, and the floodgates of the heavens were opened. [12]And rain fell on the earth forty days and forty nights."*

When God made the miracle of a world-wide flood possible, He didn't just use rain. He opened the vents at the bottom of the oceans so that the water would rise from this source also. The earth is 70% water, and the Creator used it all at this sad and devastating event.

The fossil evidence backs up what the Bible says about the world-wide flood. Fossils of ocean animals are continually being discovered all over the world, even on the highest of mountains!

The Animals

The animals God rescued from the flood to repopulate the earth are mentioned repeatedly in Genesis 6, 7 and 8. They are first mentioned in 6:19-20.

> [19]*You are to bring into the ark two of all living creatures, male and female, to keep them alive with you.* [20]*Two of every kind of bird, of every kind of animal and of every kind of creature that moves along the ground will come to you to be kept alive.*

People often ask how many animals were saved on the ark and how they all could fit. The number of animals was determined by how many were needed to effectively repopulate the earth after the flood. Verse 20 above used the word "kind," the same term God used in Genesis 1 and 2 to describe which animals He originally created. God said that a male and female of each "kind" of animal were needed. As explained in Chapter 1D, many creation scientists believe that "kind" is close to today's taxonomical category called "family." So "kind" refers to a group of animals which can produce offspring together. Examples of the "kinds" are dogs (Canidae), cats (Felidae), and bears (Ursidae). God put into the DNA of each "kind" of animal all the information necessary to produce a wide variety of species.

God didn't need a pair of red wolves, a pair of arctic fox, a pair of African wild dog, and a pair of German shepherds on the ark. He only needed one pair of dogs. From this one pair came all the different species of dogs that repopulated the earth.

God didn't need a pair of lions, a pair of leopards, a pair of bobcats, and a pair of house cats on the ark. He only needed one pair of cats. From it came all the different species of cats.

God only needed one pair of the bear kind, elephant kind, sheep kind, kangaroo kind, and horse kind. This reality greatly reduced the total number of animals needed to join Noah on the ark.

It's also important to realize that none of the aquatic animals needed to be protected in the ark. Enough of them would survive on their own.

So how many animals needed to be on the ark? Here is how some creation scientists estimate the number.[30] The list below includes animals which are extinct now, but through fossils, are known to have existed before the flood. It also includes God's requirement of seven pairs of certain animals. The arthropods are not included in the list because, though they would require great care, they would take up very little space.

- 248 "kinds" of amphibians X 2 = 496
- 320 "kinds" of reptiles X 2 for most, and X 14 for others = 928. This includes the many types of dinosaurs known to have existed.
- 284 "kinds" of birds X 14 for most, and X 2 for others = 3,676
- 78 "kinds" of synapsids X 2 = 156
- 468 "kinds" of mammals X 2 for most, and X 14 for others = 1,488

The total of 1,398 "kinds" of animals multiplied by 2 or 14 brings the total number of animals on the ark with Noah to 6,744. For the purpose of simplicity, this number is rounded up to 6,800. As mentioned in the section on the ark, there was plenty of room for this number of animals, especially considering that God would have sent the younger, smaller pairs of each animal "kind". Each pair of smaller animals were safely in their cages, while each pair of larger animals were safely in their pens.

God was concerned about the food and care of the animals while they were housed on the ark, so He told Noah "to take every kind of food that is to be eaten and store it away as food for you and for them" (Genesis 6:21). Noah did as God commanded and had plenty of room to categorize and store the food for the animals for about a year.

One last question needs to be answered. How is it, that at just the right time before the flood begins, all these 6,800 animals begin to line up outside the ark, almost as if to ask permission to board? The

Bible hints at the answer several times. As God was preparing Noah to understand all that would happen, He told him in Genesis 6:20,

> *"Two of every kind of bird, of every kind of animal, and of every kind of creature that moves along the ground will come to you to be kept alive."*

God promised that these designated animals "will come to you to be kept alive." God was telling Noah, "I'll take care of this. You just get the ark ready for the animals."

God kept His promise. In Genesis 7:15, as the waters were about to flood the earth, we read that "Pairs of all creatures that have the breath of life in them came to Noah and entered the ark." This was God's doing. He has an intimate relationship with the animals He created; when He calls them, either to carry out an assignment or simply to be saved from a flood, they gladly obey. As we imagine that long line of obedient animals marching by twos into the ark, we should also see God's dominance over the animals and His great love for them.

From approximately 6,800 animals God repopulated the animal kingdom. From these animals have come all the species which are known today. How great the animals must have felt as they got off that ark! Try to imagine that as you read the following passage from Genesis 8:15-17.

> [15]*Then God said to Noah,* [16]*"Come out of the ark, you and your wife and your sons and their wives.* [17]*Bring out every kind of living creature that is with you – the birds, the animals, and all the creatures that move along the ground – so they can multiply on the earth and be fruitful and increase in number upon it."*

Finally free to stretch their legs, run, fly, explore, hunt and breed! God had kept His promise. Not only had He saved the human race, He had also rescued His cherished animals.

The God of the Flood

What do you think? Did God behave badly as He unleashed the global flood as judgment on man's sin? Was this a divine temper tantrum? Should someone scold God for being so mean? Many people would say yes.

On the other hand, was He too gracious in that He saved both the human race and the animal kingdom from utter destruction? Was He an over-lenient judge, letting the guilty party off too easily?

As mentioned earlier in this chapter, God's punishment on human sin flows out of both His holiness and His justice. Think of His holiness first. There is no sin in Him. We are so full of sin that we can't even imagine sinlessness. But in Him is no pride, egotism, selfishness, lying, lust, or laziness; rather, only humility, love, patience, self-sacrifice, helpfulness, and friendliness.

Now think about God's justice. He is always fair so every sin of every sinner must receive its just punishment. As Judge of you and me and all people, He won't take a bribe, nor will His sentence be excessive or lenient. His judgments are always true and correct.

Was the Great Flood fair on God's part? Of course it was, because He is holy, and human sin, evil, violence, and abuse are all unacceptable to Him. In His justice, He punishes human sin perfectly. It may seem radical to us, but the Creator God, in His holiness and justice, always judges fairly.

There's more. The holy and just God who sent His judgment on human sin by means of the Great Flood is also profoundly merciful. Though we don't deserve it, He wants as many sinners as possible to live with Him forever in heaven. That's why He sent His Son Jesus to save us from the condemnation of our sin. On the cross, Jesus bore the great flood of God's wrath and punishment in the place of all us sinners. Now whoever believes in Jesus receives His full and free forgiveness and finds that eternal condemnation has been replaced with eternal life. He is an astounding God: totally holy and just, yet profoundly loving and merciful!

Conclusion

If at the time of the Great Flood God had only been interested in saving humanity, He would have told Noah to build a little bitty ark. But that was not the case. When a family loads up its car for a trip, it would never forget the pets. When God loaded up Noah's ark at the time of the flood, He couldn't forget His animals. God puts such importance on them that He can't imagine Planet Earth without them. In rescuing the animals, God shows that He is *The Greatest Animal Lover!*

CHAPTER 4

SPECIAL ASSIGNMENTS

Bible Times

One of the ways we humans show each other trust and respect is when we permit others to participate in our projects. Repeatedly in Bible times, God does exactly that with the animals He created. He gives them special tasks, enabling them to participate in different activities which move His will forward in the world of humans. Here are a few examples.

Ravens Feed Elijah in I Kings 17:1-6

Elijah was one of God's prophets to His Old Testament people sometime around 875 – 848 BC. It was a dangerous time to be a prophet. Elijah was called to speak God's Word during the reign of King Ahab and his wicked wife, Jezebel.

In I Kings 17, we find Elijah on one of his first assignments. God sends him to confront evil King Ahab and announce that because he is promoting the false god Baal to the people of Israel, God is going to withhold all rain from the area. It won't rain again until God, through Elijah, says so. This is especially embarrassing to Ahab, because his false god Baal is supposed to be the god of rain clouds and fertile land.

Ahab is furious. Elijah is immediately placed on Ahab's hit list and must get out of town (Samaria), and get out fast! Ahab's men will be trying to track him down everywhere.

Not to worry. God has a plan to keep Elijah safe even in the midst of Ahab's murderous threats. He guides His prophet to a very secluded ravine east of the Jordan River, where no one will find him. Water is flowing in the ravine, so no problem with fresh water.

But what about food? Elijah still has to eat! God tells Elijah not to fret saying, "I have ordered the ravens to feed you there" (verse 4b). Elijah probably wonders how in the world ravens will provide him with food. Verse 6 simply says, "The ravens brought him bread and meat in the morning, and bread and meat in the evening."

We'd love to have more details, right? How many ravens participated? Was there a morning crew and an evening crew? Where did they get the bread and meat? Did they drop it near Elijah, or did he take it from their beaks? Was the meat already cooked? Did it bother Elijah to eat bread that just fell from a raven's beak? In his loneliness, did Elijah talk to the ravens in a similar way that we talk to our dogs, cats, and birds? We wish we would know more, but we don't.

So why did God choose the ravens? Keil and Delitzsch give two possibilities.[31] First, since no humans knew where Elijah was, nobody could betray his location to King Ahab. Ravens are really good at zipping the lip, or beak in this case. Second, this type of miraculous provision would encourage Elijah to put his trust in the Lord in preparation for more dangerous situations with King Ahab.

We do know that God could have provided food for Elijah in some other way. Not long after this incident God provides for Elijah through a poor widow (I Kings 17:7-16). But at this specific time,

God chose to show His love and provision to his prophet through the ravens. You see, God loves honoring His created animals with special assignments.

Just an observation: I'm sure that Elijah's ravens enjoyed their role ("I'm bringing dinner!") more than the quail enjoyed their role ("I am dinner!") when God provided manna and quail for His people as they wandered in the desert (Exodus 16).

Do you think God still provides for human needs today through animals? We'll talk more about this later.

Here are additional interesting facts about these wonderful birds called ravens.

- Ravens are mentioned 11 times in the Bible.
- Ravens are considered to be among the smartest of all animals. If you wish to understand more about the intelligence of ravens, please google a Hollywood star named "Jimmy the Raven."
- Ravens are capable of imitating human speech and mimicking many other sounds.
- Ravens are extremely playful.
- Ravens are very gifted fliers. In addition to soaring and diving, they are known to do acrobatic summersaults in the air!
- Ravens mate for life and usually use the same nest year after year.
- Rescued ravens, in many cases, make wonderful pets for bird-lovers.

A Donkey Speaks God's Word in Numbers 22

This example of God giving an animal a special assignment takes place near the end of Moses' life, probably around the year 1405 BC. The Children of Israel are finishing their 40 years of wandering in the deserts of the Sinai Peninsula. There are only a few enemies standing in the way of their entry into the Promised Land of Canaan.

Balak, King of Moab, wants to attack Israel, but fears defeat. He sends for Balaam, a Babylonian diviner who is known to be able to put curses on enemy peoples. At first, Balaam refuses to go and curse Israel, but God is going to use this pagan clairvoyant for the good of His people. On a second invitation from King Balak, God tells Balaam to accept the job Balak is offering.

As Balaam journeys from Babylonia to Moab, he is riding his beloved donkey. They have been together for many years. Three times during the trip, his donkey sees an angel with its sword drawn. Each time, the donkey leaves the path in fear, and each time, Balaam beats his donkey for stubbornly veering off the trail.

Then God miraculously gives the donkey the ability to talk with her owner (22: 28). She says to Balaam, "What have I done to you to make you beat me these three times?" But Balaam is still angry at the donkey and threatens to kill her because he himself has not yet seen the angel with its drawn sword. In verse 30, the donkey asks Balaam, "Am I not your own donkey, which you have always ridden to this day? Have I been in the habit of doing this to you?" Balaam, starting to be reasonable, says "No," and God opens his eyes so he can see the angel in the path.

Now the angel speaks to Balaam (verses 32-35). The angel tells him, (1) "You shouldn't have beaten your poor donkey," (2) "I was here to oppose you because of your evil intentions toward God's people," and (3) "If the donkey had not turned aside, I would have killed you and spared the donkey!" Balaam understands the wrong he has done and will now go to Moab and pronounce blessings on God's people instead of curses. Once again, we see that God entrusts His animals with significant tasks!

Here are some interesting applications we might glean from this miracle in which God uses a donkey to enlighten a pagan medium.

First, God can enable animals to talk when He so chooses. Some Bible scholars believe that all animals had this ability before the fall into sin.

Second, the donkey's words hint that she understood that she and her master belonged together ("Am I not your own donkey?"). Do you think that many of our pets understand this idea of belonging together?

Third, the donkey's words expressed her faithfulness as a beast of burden to her master ("Am I not your own donkey, which you have always ridden to this day?"). Do you think our pets appreciate the concept of faithfulness as they relate to us?

Fourth, the donkey's words ask for justice and fair treatment ("What have I done to you to make you beat me these three times?"). Do you think that all animals bear the desire to be treated fairly?

Here are some fascinating facts about donkeys.

- Donkeys get depressed when alone. They need other animals around them to be happy.
- Donkeys have amazing memories. They can remember places, animals, and humans for up to 25 years.
- Donkeys love rolling on the ground. It is their favorite pastime!
- Donkeys have the shape of a cross in their coat that begins between their shoulders and runs down their spine.
- A female horse and a male donkey produce mules. A male horse and a female donkey produce hinnies.

A Great Fish Redirects a Wayward Prophet in Jonah 1:17-2:10

This third example is about God's love for people who do not yet know Him as the true God, and about His salvation through faith in His Son. God calls the prophet Jonah (800-750 BC) to go to the enemy city of Nineveh (in today's country of Iraq) to give its people a chance to hear about the true God, repent of their sins, and be saved.

Jonah, however, has a rebellious streak in him. He thinks God is all wrong about showing love to the enemy. Jonah will have nothing to do with it! He gets on a ship thinking he is sneaking away from God and avoiding His call to go and share the Word of God with the Ninevites. Bad idea! God sends a Mediterranean storm which threatens the lives of all on board. Jonah confesses that he is the cause of the storm, and hesitantly, the crew throws him overboard, which should have been the end of Jonah.

But God has other plans. He wants to give Jonah a second chance to obey his missionary call. He miraculously prepares a huge fish to swallow Jonah. Surprisingly, the prophet is able to breathe and stay alive inside this special fish. He has time to do some serious self-reflection and realizes that though he was drowning, God rescued him in this miraculous way. He praises the Lord for delivering him and recognizes God's power in his life. Three days later, the great fish vomits Jonah onto a beach, and so begins his second chance to proclaim God's message to the people of Nineveh.

What an incredible God the Creator is, and what a surprising relationship He has with the animals He created! The account begins with "But the Lord provided a great fish" (1:17) and ends with "and the Lord commanded the fish, and it vomited Jonah onto dry land" (2:10). God orchestrated Jonah's rescue from beginning to end, but He chose to accomplish the miracle through a special fish.

As in the cases of the ravens and the donkey, so also in the case of the great fish, God didn't have to use animals. He could have worked His will through other means, but He didn't. He chose to do it through His created animals showing them His fondness and respect. He is *The Greatest Animal Lover!*

In addition to these three examples, God gave special assignments to other animals throughout Bible times. In each case, God was confirming the value He places on the animals He created and loves.

Today

Today God continues to honor animals by giving them special assignments or roles. One role is to provide for the needs of humans. God assigns sheep, llamas, and other animals to supply us with wool for clothing; the caterpillar of the silk moth to furnish us with silk; chickens to deliver eggs; cows and goats to provide milk and cheese;

and bees to produce honey. This is just a short list. Can you think of other examples?

Another assignment God gives to animals is to entertain us. My wife and I recently took our grandkids to the San Diego Zoo Safari. The animals entertained us all day. Lorikeets drank from cups in our hands and young male elephants playfully roughhoused in their watering hole. Most exciting was seeing a young cheetah named Majani chasing a toy at 70 mph! As she ran by the crowd, everyone was gasping in disbelief. Whether at zoos, animal water parks, rodeos, horse races, safaris, or circuses, we love to be entertained by animals. As they fulfill God's assignment, they do a great job!

God also gives many animals the task of participating in the maintenance of the planet itself. God assigns dung beetles to clean up millions of tons of animal feces around the world. There are thousands of species of dung beetles, but all of them serve as poop janitors. Some eat droppings from any animal; others are fussy eaters and will only eat dung from their favorite animal. With their super sensitive antennae, they can "smell" fresh poop from far away. If it weren't for the dung beetle, many of the grasslands of Africa could no longer sustain life, as they would be covered with a thick layer of excrement. But with the presence of the dung beetle, huge herds of wildebeest or zebras can defecate all they want without damaging the grass. God's grassland janitors are happily about their assignment, sometimes even before the poop hits the ground!

In addition, God gives many animals the assignment of participating in the maintenance of life on the planet. This can be seen in animals which God has designed to be pollinators. Pollination is required for a flowering plant to have successful fertilization which produces the growth of seeds and fruit. Although some plants depend on wind or water to transfer pollen from one flower to the next, approximately 90% of all plant species are dependent on animals for pollination.[32] Some of the animals which God designed as pollinators are nectar bats; birds, such as hummingbirds; and insects, such as bees, wasps, bumblebees, moths, butterflies, and beetles. In many cases, the symbiosis between the plant and its animal pollinator is essential for both. The plant can't reproduce without the pollinator, and the pollinator can't survive without the plant's nectar. The best explanation for this delicate interdependence is that it came about through the creative act of a brilliant Designer God!

Horses

For thousands of years, God has assigned horses to provide power for humans. Horses are much stronger than humans; a man can produce 75 watts of power per hour, but a horse can produce 750! God has assigned horses to plow our fields, carry our loads, and provide transportation. In WWI, millions of horses helped do the work of war.

Today, horses still dazzle us with their beauty, strength, speed, and companionship. Many of us get great pleasure out of seeing them race. Some of our subcultures are built around breeding horses that can impress us with their speed. They perform beautifully in many shows and play a key role in rodeos. For many people, horses are man's best friend!

One of the most surprising yet delightful ways that God uses horses today is to provide a healthy and healing presence for humans. The restoration which takes place by being with a trained horse is called equine therapy. Healing through horses is a quickly growing type of therapy around the world.

Humans can find healing in horses because God has given them special characteristics. First, since horses are flight animals, they are hypersensitive. They notice and evaluate a huge amount of data all around them. This can include the physical, mental, and emotional state of the humans near them. Second, horses are nonjudgmental. One gets to start with a clean slate in their presence. Third, though very big and strong, they are also gentle and responsive.

Though equine therapy may take place in an informal setting, it often occurs under the care of medical professionals. If the patient is struggling with mental or emotional issues, the team will include a trained horse, a certified equine specialist, and a certified psychotherapist. If the patient's challenges are more physical, the team will include a certified physical or occupational therapist.

In equine therapy, the patient may interact with the horse in different ways. These may include simply being close to, touching and hugging, grooming, walking with, or riding on the horse. The patient may also be blessed by preparing the horse for a rider or learning to give the horse orders.

Equine therapy has proven to be helpful for a wide range of illnesses including attention deficit, eating disorders, trauma disorders, substance abuse, anxiety, autism, dementia, depression, bipolar disorder, post-traumatic stress disorder (PTSD), traumatic brain disorders, and many other mental, emotional, and physical challenges.

Here are some of the benefits of equine therapy: growth in communication and relationship skills, impulse control, trust, a growing sense of self-worth and self-confidence, stress reduction, emotional awareness, empathy, and flexibility.

If this information is new to you, and you know someone who could be blessed through equine therapy, please google the subject to find a nearby institution which provides this special kind of God-designed healing.

Dogs

Maybe the animal to which God gives the most responsibilities is the dog. Throughout history, and throughout the world, dogs have been recognized for their loyal friendship. This is a God-given assignment which gives us a glimpse of what the human-animal relationship was like in the Garden of Eden before the fall into sin.

The acute sense of smell that God has given to dogs is a great blessing to humans. Dogs' noses aid our police force either by tracking innocent captives or hunting and capturing bad guys. Imagine how many arrests would never have taken place if not for our K-9 specialists! Our drug enforcement agencies rely heavily on a dog's ability to sniff out illegal drugs. Our drug problems would be much worse without dogs! Our antiterrorism and military personnel depend on dogs to sniff out bombs. Think about how many thousands of people have been saved from being blown to bits because a dog discovered the bomb in time! I believe that dogs get a lot of satisfaction by fulfilling their God-given, nose-related tasks.

Because of their sense of smell, dogs are of great value to humans. But of even more value to us is their heart, that is, their God-given ability to provide comfort, hope, and healing when we need it the most. Dogs trained in crisis response have brought untold comfort and hope to people suffering in the aftermath of hurricanes, tornadoes, floods, bombings, and shootings. Therapy dogs bring healing to those struggling in hospitals, nursing homes, Alzheimer's units, and addiction rehab facilities. Through animal-assisted therapy (AAT), dogs provide encouragement to patients striving to recover from strokes, surgeries, or concussions. Service dogs give their owners, struggling with different mental and emotional challenges, the ability to move forward in life with more confidence. Guide dogs enable their blind owners to navigate with more freedom and assurance. The list of ways that God uses dogs to bless us seems endless! Thank God for dogs!

Biomimicry

God also gives animals the task of teaching humans how to improve their technology by learning from the marvelous design God built into the animals. Biomimicry is the science of providing solutions to human problems by imitating the design and engineering found in the world of plants and animals.[33]

Have you noticed that at the moment of being bitten by a mosquito, you usually don't feel it? That's because the mosquito proboscis has seven moving parts which enable it to penetrate our skin with little or no pain. Scientists have been studying the mosquito proboscis for years now and are designing new hypodermic needles which are less painful as they enter our skin.

Mussels produce a powerful water proof glue which enables them to stick to almost any surface. This glue also repairs itself if the bond is broken. Scientists are examining this glue in order to make some of our own! From these studies, new glues are being created for repairing boats and maybe even sealing surgical incisions.

Wind turbine technology is being blessed by two animals. The tubercles on the front end of the fins of the humpback whale are imitated to produce wind turbine blades which turn with less wind resistance. Also, the figure 8 motion of the wings of the hummingbird is being copied to create more effective wind turbine blade movement.

Aren't you astounded by the echolocation used by bats and dolphins? Scientists are now imitating this technology to make high-tech canes for blind people. These canes notify the person of danger by vibrating when an object is in their path.

Right now, scientists are upgrading our technology by studying and imitating spider silk, hagfish slime, gecko toes, shark denticles, lobster eyes, and kingfisher beaks. Why are animals able to aid us with their complex design? Because they were created by an awesome Designer, and He loves it when animals serve us humans in so many ways!

In this chapter we have seen that both in Bible times and today God gives animals special assignments. This is evidence that He loves and admires them. He truly is *The Greatest Animal Lover*!

CHAPTER 5

POINTING TO THE SAVIOR

Many people criticize the Old Testament animal sacrifices. They ask, "How could the God who created and loves animals permit them to be slaughtered as sacrifices? Wasn't the Old Testament animal sacrificial system a simple case of humans abusing animals for religious purposes?"

Both of these tough questions are easily answered when one understands the significance and importance of these God-ordained sacrifices. God designed them to help His Old Testament people understand and believe the most important concepts of human existence. These concepts include the following:

1. The reality of our sin in that we daily fail to live up to God's high moral standards
2. The profound guilt which our sin imposes on us before a holy and righteous God
3. The just punishment of our human sin which is physical, spiritual and eternal death

4. The extreme importance of on-going repentance and confession of sin

5. The amazing grace (undeserved love) of God, through which He offers to us and all sinners the full and free forgiveness of our sins simply by believing in a Substitute.

When a person understands how crucial these truths are for the salvation of sinners like us, the legitimacy of the Old Testament animal sacrificial system becomes obvious. This was not a case of humans abusing animals for petty religious reasons. These sacrifices were commanded by the God whose love for lost sinners supersedes His love for animals. They were a way in which God helped His Old Testament people be saved by believing, not in the animal sacrificed, but in the future Messiah/Savior, whose death would be the all-sufficient sacrifice for everyone's sins. (The word "Messiah" is an Old Testament term referring to the future Savior of the world.)

In this chapter we will look at the first animal sacrifice and the animal sacrifices which God prescribed for His Old Testament people.

The First Animal Sacrifice

The first example of an animal being sacrificed for the sake of sinners is found at the end of Genesis 3. Adam and Eve had sinned and felt guilty before God. They no longer felt comfortable being naked before Him, so they covered their shame by sewing together fig leaves (Genesis 3:7).

Later, as they were being expelled from the Garden of Eden, God showed His compassion for them. Verse 21 says, "The Lord God made garments of skin for Adam and his wife and clothed them." The only place God could have gotten these "garments of skin" was from an animal. Because of man's sin and God's judgment on it, death was now entering the animal kingdom, as well as the world of humans.

The new clothes for Adam and Eve were not just to protect them from the elements. These garments of skin showed that God was covering their shame and forgiving their sin, which had to be punished by death. However, death did not fall on Adam and Eve, but rather on a substitute, the animal from which their new clothing came. The dead animal provided new garments which reminded them of God's promise (Genesis 3:15) to send a Messiah/Savior who would die for the forgiveness of their sins, and also that they should place their faith in this future Savior.

God created, loved, admired, and cared for this animal, so I believe its sacrificial death brought sadness to God's heart. But in another way, this death brought Him satisfaction. He knew that Adam and Eve understood His forgiving love as they put on those garments of skin and put their faith in the future Messiah/Savior, who would die for their sins. Remember, nothing is more important to God than sinful human beings being saved from the condemnation of their sins by believing in His Son, Jesus Christ, the Savior of the world. Animal sacrifices in the Old Testament were intended for this purpose: to guide the participants to put their trust in the future Messiah/Savior, the One called "the Lamb of God," for the forgiveness of their sins.

Types of Animal Sacrifices

In the first five chapters of Leviticus, four of the most common animal sacrifices are described. The first is the burnt offering, also called a holocaust. This sacrifice had two purposes: to find forgiveness and atonement for unintentional sins and to express total commitment or surrender to God and His will. The animal sacrificed could be a bull, ram, or male bird. After the sacrifice, the whole carcass of the animal would be burned completely.

The second is the fellowship offering. The significance of this sacrifice went beyond obtaining forgiveness and the thankful expression of devotion to God. It included taking some of the meat home to celebrate God's goodness and salvation with family and friends. The animal sacrificed could be an ox, bull, lamb, or goat. Some of the meat was consumed by fire, some assigned to the priests, and some was taken home for the fellowship celebration.

The third and fourth sacrifices were the <u>sin offering</u> and the <u>guilt offering</u>. These were similar mandatory sacrifices to receive forgiveness and cleansing for certain sins. The guilt offering, though, included the requirement of restitution to the offended party. The animal sacrificed could be a bull, goat, lamb, dove, or pigeon. Some of the meat would be consumed by fire, some eaten by the priests, and some taken outside the city gates to be burned.

All Sacrifices Pointed to Jesus

God wanted all of His Old Testament people to be able to participate in these comforting sacrifices no matter what their socio-economic status. Wealthier people might have to bring an ox or a bull, those from the middle-class a goat or a sheep, and the poor a dove or a pigeon. But what each of these sacrificed animals had in common was that they were all pictures of the future Messiah/Savior, Jesus Christ. To those people bringing their animal to be sacrificed, God was not saying, "Believe in the death of this animal for your forgiveness." God was saying, "This animal is to remind you what your future Savior will do for you. Believe in Him!"

The sacrificial animal served as a reminder of the future Messiah/Savior in several ways. First, the animal had to be perfect, without any kind of sickness. The Biblical phrase "without defect" (Leviticus 1:3) indicates that this animal was in a sense "morally superior" to the sinner. The perfection of the animal sacrificed was a picture of Jesus. As the Son of God made Man, He never sinned once, not in thought, word, or deed. Jesus could only serve as our Savior if He were sinless, and He was. I Peter 1:18-19 describes it like this:

> *[18] For you know that it was not with perishable things such as silver or gold that you were redeemed from*

> *the empty ways of life handed down to you from your forefathers, [19]but with the precious blood of Christ, a lamb without blemish or defect.*

Second, the sacrificed animal was pointing its owner to the future Messiah/Savior by becoming the owner's substitute in two senses. It became guilty of the owner's sin, and it was punished in the owner's place. This double substitution is exactly what Jesus did for us sinners. He took our sin and guilt upon himself, becoming the guilty one in our place. Then, as our Substitute, He was punished for our sins.

Third, the sacrificed animal reminded its owner of Jesus as it was slaughtered, and its blood was presented as evidence of death. In God's eyes, death is the just punishment of our sin (Genesis 2:17). This is why much attention was paid to the blood of the sacrificed animal, for it meant that the animal was truly dead and the sinner's punishment fully paid. Each bloody sacrifice was a picture of what would happen to Jesus, the Savior. Becoming our Substitute in sin, guilt, and punishment, He would be slaughtered on the cross of Calvary. His blood flowed freely from the wounds of the whip, the crown of thorns, the nails, and finally the spear. He truly died and did so in our place and for our sin. His saving actions were prophesied at each animal sacrifice. The only way in which the sacrificed animals failed to paint a picture of Jesus' saving ministry is that not one of them rose from the dead!

Fourth, the sacrificed animal pointed its owner to Jesus when he was declared forgiven by the priest. A frequently repeated statement in the description of these animal sacrifices is found in Leviticus 4:20, "In this way the priest will make atonement for them, and they will be forgiven." Atonement here means to be at one with God. Sin separated the owner from God, but the animal sacrifice and the owner's faith in the future Messiah/Savior brought forgiveness, making him at one with God again. This emphasis on forgiveness and atonement is a picture of what Jesus would accomplish in His life, death, and resurrection. Those who believe in Him find forgiveness, peace with God, and the sure hope of eternal life.

In a sense it was a privilege for each animal to die because it was serving both God and God's people, enabling them to find forgiveness not in the animal itself, but in the future Savior whom each animal foreshadowed. Even though every animal sacrifice was terribly sad, there was honor for the animal as it pointed sinners to their Savior, the Messiah, Jesus Christ.

Reviewing the Details and Meaning of the Burnt Offering

Now we will walk through the animal sacrifice called the burnt offering by imagining ourselves to be members of an Old Testament family. On the basis of Leviticus 1:1-17 and 6:8-13, we will observe five distinct steps in the sacrifice.

The father of our family is concerned about the sins we have been committing. We are all sorry and want to be assured of God's forgiveness and rededicate our lives to Him. As a middle-class family, we may offer either a male goat or a male sheep. Our dad chooses our healthiest little lamb. The children have begun to treat him as their pet, but we want to offer the best we have to the Lord. (The perfection of the animal is the first picture of Jesus the Savior.)

As we start walking toward the Tent of Meeting (Tabernacle) with our little lamb in tow, we are both sad and excited. We are sad because our favorite lamb is going to die but joyful knowing that God's forgiveness and peace are going to be renewed in our lives. We will be rededicating every aspect of our lives to our wonderful God.

First, we present our lamb to the priest at the entrance of the Tent of Meeting. This step basically says, "Hello Lord, we are coming into your presence today. We know that our sinfulness does not mix with your holiness. But look, Lord, we are bringing a substitute just like you said. Please accept it in our place."

Second, our father lays his hands on the head of the lamb and confesses our sins. This step is to transfer our sin and guilt onto our substitute. Now, according to God's merciful plan, it will receive the punishment of our sins in our place. Here we are saying to the Lord,

"Please let your punishment for our sins fall on this lamb and your forgiveness on us." (This is another picture of Jesus the Savior, who would take our sin and guilt upon Himself, becoming the "sinner," laden with our sins.)

Third, we enter into the outer area of the Tent of Meeting, and the lamb is sacrificed, either by our father or by the priest. The prayer at this moment might be, "Heavenly Father, we know that because of our sin we deserve to die. But look, by your grace, this animal is being killed in our place. Thank you for letting our punishment fall on it and not on us!" (This is the third picture of Jesus the Savior, who would suffer and die in our place.)

Fourth, the priest catches the blood of our lamb in a special container. Our family now steps aside while the priest sprinkles some of the blood on the Bronze Altar at the entrance of the Tent of Meeting. In this way the priest indicates, "Look at this blood, Lord. It is the proof that this family's substitute has indeed died and paid the price of their sin. Your just punishment has been carried out in their substitute." This may be the time when the priest declares our family forgiven and at peace with God. (This is the final picture of Jesus, because all who believe in Him receive the forgiveness of their sins.)

The first goal of the animal sacrifice (burnt offering) has now been accomplished. What our future Messiah/Savior will do for us has been pre-enacted in the sacrifice of our little lamb. We believe in that future Savior. We have God's full and free forgiveness and are at one with Him once again (atonement). Out of thankfulness, our family now wants to rededicate ourselves to this loving God.

Fifth, we now watch as the priest skins our lamb. The priest will be allowed to keep the skin for bedding or clothing. He cuts our sacrificed lamb into pieces and washes certain portions in preparation for burning. He puts the pieces of our lamb on the very hot grill of the Bronze Altar and in just a few minutes, they are totally consumed. As all of this is happening, our father might be praying out loud, "O Lord, we thank You for renewing your undeserved forgiveness in our lives. Your mercy is overwhelming. As our sacrificed lamb is cut into pieces, we ask, Lord, that You would take every aspect of our lives and use us for your glory. As our lamb is totally consumed by the fire, may your Holy Spirit consume us, not just part of us, but all of us. Out of deep gratitude for your undeserved forgiveness, we now dedicate every aspect of our lives to You. Use us as you wish. We are totally yours!" Then our family walks back home, full of the joy of God's forgiveness and salvation.

It is evident that the animal sacrifices were of great spiritual value for God's Old Testament people. Their sacrificial animals reminded them of the seriousness of their sin, the amazing grace of God, and the importance of trusting in the future Messiah/Savior for forgiveness. Therefore, it was an honor for each sacrificed animal to point to the coming Savior.

According to God's plan, all animal sacrifices ended abruptly on Good Friday, when Jesus, the Lamb of God who takes away the sin of the world, was sacrificed for you, me and sinners of all time. The honor is all His!

CHAPTER 6

REFERRALS

Jesus and various Bible authors often refer to animals to illustrate important truths. It is fun to see the connection between each animal mentioned and the life lesson taught.

Ants and Hard Work

In the Book of Proverbs, the authors often refer to animals as they teach about wisdom. Twice, in 6:6-8 and 30:24-25, they use ants to teach about the wisdom of hard work and saving for the future. Look at the first one with me:

> ⁶Go to the ant, you sluggard; consider its ways and be wise! ⁷ It has no commander, no overseer or ruler, ⁸yet it stores its provisions in summer and gathers its food at harvest.

A sluggard is a person who is lazy and sleeps excessively yet complains when something is lacking. This attitude or lifestyle is against God's will. He is a hard worker, and under normal circumstances, wants us to be active, hard-working, productive individuals. Solomon sends sluggards to watch and learn from the ants. The lazy person will gain much from them, since they are not afraid to exert themselves and are willing to work long and hard. They belong to a colony and know how to work as a team. During the work day, they don't need to have a superior watching over their shoulder to see if they are doing their part; they do this naturally. They work smart and store up food for skinny times.

If the lazy person does indeed learn from the ants and adopt their lifestyle, what a change would occur! Maybe children who are lazy at home and at school, and employees who are lazy at work, need to take the "Go to the Ants" course.

What an honor for ants! God uses them to teach us humans how to live our lives wisely!

Birds and Reducing Worry and Fear

In the Sermon on the Mount, Jesus teaches about worry because He knows how it can sap the joy out of life. He wants us to trust Him and not fret. In the paragraphs about worry (Matthew 6:25-34), Jesus makes several practical points. First, life is bigger than material stuff (verse 25). Second, worrying is worthless; it won't help you get what you want (verse 27). Third, remember you have a heavenly Father who knows your needs (verse 32). Fourth, instead of worrying about tomorrow, focus on today (verse 34). In verse 26 Jesus adds this thought:

> Look at the birds of the air; they do not sow or reap or
> store away in barns, and yet your heavenly Father feeds
> them. Are you not much more valuable than they?

Jesus encourages worry-warts to watch and learn from the birds of the air. They are active but stress free as they hunt for food, build nests, and feed their young. Many perching songbirds spend a good part of the day just singing! Birds don't need to plant, harvest, and store their food like we do, yet under normal circumstances, they have all the food they need. Why? Because God is watching over them and providing for their needs. Here's the lesson: If our God takes care of providing sufficient food for the birds in our neighborhood, won't He much more provide for our needs, since we are human beings created in His image? And if that's true, why worry? Why not just trust Him?

Later, in Matthew 10, Jesus commissions His 12 apostles to preach, teach, and do miracles in His name. Jesus sees that some of them are afraid of being sent on this mission. Their fear is understandable, as this is a new experience for them, and they know there will be enemies in their path. Jesus prepares them for the task with this advice: First, don't worry about finances (verses 9-10). Second, if one group rejects your message, move on to the next opportunity (verses 11-16). Third, if you get arrested and need to speak before powerful leaders, don't worry; My Spirit will guide you in what to say (verses 17-20). Fourth, don't be surprised if enemies of the gospel persecute you. If they treat Me badly, they will treat you worse (verses 21-25)! Fifth, pay more attention to God's will than to the threats of men (verse 28).

Finally, Jesus tries to calm their fears with these words:

> 29Are not two sparrows sold for a penny? Yet not one of them will fall to the ground apart from the will of your Father. 30And even the very hairs of your head are all numbered. 31So don't be afraid; you are worth more than many sparrows.

These words of Jesus also apply to us today. He knows that fear, like worry, can make life miserable. He doesn't want us to be afraid of failure, the future, danger, illness, or loss. He wants us to live with confidence, trusting in Him. That's why He spoke of the common sparrows. They don't have dazzling colors or sing beautiful songs. You'd go broke trying to sell them because in people's eyes they have little value. But they are of such great value to the God who created them that not one little bird can fall to the ground without its Creator being aware of it. If that is true of God's care for a simple little sparrow, how much more will He be involved in our lives, protecting and guiding us in everything we do. In God's eyes we are of greater value than sparrows, for He created us in His image and sent His Son to die for our sins. When fear takes hold of us, we only need to think about God's care for sparrows. This will reassure us of His great love and involvement in our lives. Remembering God's care for sparrows can be a fear-buster for us.

What an honor for little birds! Jesus refers to them as He instructs us to put aside worry and fear.

Hens and Jesus' Saving Ministry

One of the sad realities that Jesus dealt with was the way many of His own Jewish countrymen were rejecting Him as their Messiah and Savior. He deeply desired all people to believe in Him for forgiveness and eternal life. But many of the people in Jerusalem were lost in their false religious ideas and would not believe in Him. In Luke 13:34 Jesus is lamenting this sad reality. Here is what He says:

> O Jerusalem, Jerusalem, you who kill the prophets
> and stone those sent to you, how often I have longed
> to gather your children together, as a hen gathers her
> chicks under her wings, but you were not willing!

When a mother hen senses any kind of danger, whether that of a fire, a predator, or a storm, she communicates with her chicks. They know exactly what she means and come running to her. One by one, she tucks them under her wings to hide and protect them with her life. She will willingly die before permitting any harm to her chicks.

There is a story which illustrates this truth. A fire raged through a farmer's barn, and not all the animals were able to get out. Later the farmer was walking through his burned-out barn evaluating his losses. He came upon a hen which was completely burned. With his boot, he nudged the dead hen, and suddenly, three little chicks came running out from underneath her scorched wings. They were unharmed by the fire. She had given her life for them.

When Jesus says that He wanted to gather together the people of Jerusalem like a hen gathers her chicks under her wings, He was indicating how He wanted to save them from the condemnation of their sins. The great danger for all humans is God's just punishment because of our sins. Jesus calls all of us to come running to Him at the cross, where He spreads out His nail-pierced hands and receives all of God's wrath and punishment in our place. The innocent One gives up His life for the guilty! Those of us who by faith in Him remain gathered at the foot of the cross are untouched by God's punishment. Jesus is like the hen in the barn fire and we who believe in Him are like the chicks. We go out from under Jesus' arms on the cross unharmed and forgiven of all our sins!

What an honor for all hens! Jesus explains His saving ministry by crediting their example!

Wolves and Lions and the Enemies of the Christian Faith

In the Sermon on the Mount, Jesus compares wolves to false teachers who appear to be teaching the truth but are actually cultivating a mixture of truth and falsehood. In Jesus' day, even the official religious leaders were false teachers. They were instructing people to save themselves on the basis of their own good works. This was a lie because we sinners are saved only by God's grace through faith in Jesus. The effect of false teaching is that people often believe it and end up being condemned eternally.

In view of this tragic result, Jesus used very strong language in describing false teachers. Here is how He put it in Matthew 7:15:

Watch out for false prophets. They come to you in
sheep's clothing, but inwardly they are ferocious wolves.

Jesus describes teachers who mislead as ferocious wolves dressed in "sheep's clothing" because sometimes they come across as innocent and sincere. "Ferocious wolves" indicates their lies are potentially able to lead Christians into false beliefs and ultimately cause them to lose their saving faith.

This is not to give wolves a bad name. They are remarkable, but indeed ferocious. Wolves are big, fast, strong carnivores that don't give up when chasing prey. They are highly intelligent and hunt as a pack. Their senses of sound, smell, and sight are out of this world. The strength of their bite is about twice as strong as that of a domesticated dog, and they commonly take down animals much bigger than themselves, such as deer, elk, and moose. Once the prey is taken down, they eat it all!

When you put these characteristics together, you have a ferocious animal. Jesus is saying that false teachers are also ferocious. Often, they have strong personalities and can be very convincing. They are dedicated to their distorted ideas and can deceive even mature Christians with their subtle lies. If not stopped, they can cause faithful Christians to lose their salvation. Jesus is calling Christians to do everything in their power to avoid false teachers and evaluate every teaching based on the clear Word of God, the Bible. Just as a ferocious wolf causes us much concern that needs a wise reaction, so also deceitful teachers.

What an honor for wolves! Jesus cites them as He teaches us about the great danger of false teachers.

The biggest enemy of Christians and the Christian faith is the devil. He is the most powerful demon, the evil angel of highest rank who hates God but cannot hurt Him directly. Therefore, he loves to hurt what God loves most: in general, all humans created in His image, and specifically, all believers in Jesus. Satan attempts to keep unbelievers mired in their false beliefs and desires to cause Christians to fall away from their faith. He will use any method available. Three of his favorites are intellectual doubt, religious disorientation, and moral confusion. To achieve his goals, he also uses false teachers, as noted above.

In view of who Satan is and how he works, St. Peter compares him to a lion in I Peter 5:8-9a.

> [8]Be self-controlled and alert. Your enemy the devil prowls around like a roaring lion looking for someone to devour. [9] Resist him, standing firm in the faith.

When St. Peter compares the devil to a lion, he is not saying that lions are evil. He is focusing on their strength and tenacity. Lions are huge, with males often weighing around 400 pounds. They are fast, chasing their prey at up to 50 miles per hour, and strong enough to pull down zebras and wildebeests. Lions are brilliant hunters, organizing their night time attacks with other members of their pride. They are hungry, eating up to 15 pounds of meat a day, and their roar can be heard from over four miles away.

These are some of the reasons that the Bible compares the devil to a lion. Like a lion, the devil is strong, fast, smart, hungry, and ferocious. He relentlessly works to keep doubters in unbelief and cause Christians to fall from their faith in Jesus. He aspires to drag as many people as possible to hell. One way in which the devil is not like a lion is that the lion sleeps up to 20 hours a day, but the devil never rests!

In view of having such a strong spiritual enemy, St. Peter encourages Christians to "be self-controlled and alert." This means to be on the lookout for any of the ways the devil might be tempting us to distance ourselves from Jesus as our Savior and Lord. We should daily confess our sins, trust in Jesus for His forgiveness and strength, and remember that though the devil is strong, he is no match for Jesus (I John 4:4)! That's why Jesus is also called a lion in Revelation 5:5. He ferociously defends His own!

What an honor for lions! By pointing to them, the Bible cautions us to be on guard against the attacks of the devil in our lives.

Sheep and Calves and Believers in Jesus

In the Bible, sheep are often used to describe believers in Jesus. In John 10:1-18 Jesus describes His followers as sheep and Himself as a shepherd. Look at verses 11 and 14a:

> [11]*I am the good shepherd. The good shepherd lays down his life for the sheep.*

> [14]*I am the good shepherd; I know my sheep and my sheep know me.*

Jesus compares Himself to a shepherd in two ways. In verse 14 He says that just like a shepherd, He knows His sheep. It's true that shepherds know every one of their sheep. Last January my wife and I were hiking in a rural area of the Peruvian Andes and we came across a shepherd and his large flock of sheep. We asked him how many sheep he had, and without blinking an eye he said, "One hundred and two." He didn't just know the total number, he knew each of them by name. Jesus is like that. He knows with great detail each of us who believe in Him, right down to the number of hairs on our heads (Matthew 10:30)! He knows our weaknesses and strengths, defeats and victories, sins and intentions. No one can know us or help us like Jesus.

In verse 11 Jesus says that just like a shepherd, He lays down his life for the sheep. Occasionally a shepherd dies defending his flock from a mountain lion, a bear, or a pack of wolves. This is exactly what Jesus did for us, His sheep. He put himself in the path of God's punishment for our sins and received it all in our place. He suffered and died to make possible our full and free forgiveness. Fortunately, unlike the earthly shepherds, Jesus rose again on the third day, guaranteeing our life forever with Him in heaven. What a shepherd Jesus is for us!

In addition to comparing himself to a shepherd, Jesus compares us to sheep. No offense to sheep, but this comparison is not meant to flatter us. Sheep are not the brightest bulbs on the animal chandelier. They tend to wander off and not find their way back home. They are easy prey for most predators because they don't bite, kick, or run fast. Left alone, sheep are toast.

Therefore, sheep are an accurate picture of us who believe in Jesus as our Savior. Distracted by the ways of this sinful world, we also tend to wander away from our Shepherd, Jesus. If Jesus doesn't come calling us, we might not ever get back home to Him. Like sheep, we have a dangerous predator. Remember the devil being compared to a roaring lion in I Peter 5:8? Left on our own, guess who wins? But Jesus protects us through His Word and Sacraments. He sends us His Holy Spirit to guide us. He encourages us through Christian friends. We are strong only while depending on His strength. Yes, we sheep are blessed to have Jesus as our shepherd!

What an honor for sheep! By referring to them Jesus demonstrates important truths about who we are and what we need.

The prophet Malachi compares us Christians to calves. In Malachi 4:2, he is writing about an event called "the Day of the Lord."

But for you who revere my name, the sun of righteousness will rise with healing in its wings. And you will go out and leap like calves released from the stall.

Malachi is referring both to the first coming of Jesus when He came to save us and to His Second Coming when He will usher us into the new heaven and new earth. When Malachi compares us to calves leaping upon being released from the stall, he is ultimately describing the joy that will be ours when Jesus returns. For those of us who weren't raised on a farm or ranch, it's hard to visualize this picture of calves leaping, but if you google "videos of calves leaping," you will know exactly what Malachi is expressing. When calves are set free for the first time in the spring, they are so happy they can't stop running and jumping in the field. Their action paints a picture of pure joy, which is what believers in Jesus will experience on the great Last Day when Jesus will return in glory and give us new resurrection bodies designed to live with Him forever. We will be declared innocent in the Final Judgment and welcomed into the new heaven and new earth. Our joy will be like that of calves when they are released from the stall. We will not be able to stop our joyful and thankful praise to Jesus our Savior.

What an honor for little calves! Malachi uses them to paint a picture of the joy we will experience at Jesus' Second Coming.

The End of the Prey/Predator Dynamic and Life in the New Heaven and New Earth

The prophet Isaiah lived about 700 years before the Messiah Jesus was born. In chapter 11 of his book, Isaiah is writing about this future Messiah. First, he describes who the Messiah will be (verse 1). Then he mentions some of the qualities of the Messiah (verse 2). Next Isaiah gives examples of some of His activities and achievements (verses 3-5). Finally, he describes the peace that will be accomplished by the Messiah (verses 6-9).

> *6The wolf will live with the lamb, the leopard will lie down with the goat, the calf and the lion and the yearling together; and a little child will lead them. 7The cow will feed with the bear, their young will lie down together, and the lion will eat straw like the ox. 8The infant will play near the hole of the cobra, and the young child put his hand into the viper's nest. 9They will neither harm nor destroy on all my holy mountain, for the earth will be full of the knowledge of the Lord as the waters cover the sea.*

Isaiah is using this unusual picture of animals and humans in total harmony with one another to illustrate the peace that the Messiah Jesus brings to those who believe in Him. Since He wins the forgiveness of all our sins, we have peace with God. Though we have made ourselves God's enemies because of our sin, God reconciles us to Himself through Jesus' sacrifice on the cross. What peace we have knowing that God is not angry at us but cherishes us as His own dear children! When this forgiveness-filled peace is in our hearts, it enables us to be peacemakers in our relationships with those around us. Our forgiving and peaceful lifestyle demonstrates to the world what Jesus, the Prince of Peace, has achieved in our lives.

Life in this world will never see the total fulfillment of the peaceful scene described above. That's why we believe that Isaiah is projecting what Jesus' peace will be like in the new heaven and new earth. For those of you who are less familiar with Christian doctrine, let me explain. The Bible teaches that this world will come to an end. On that Last Day several events will occur. (1) Jesus will visibly return to earth and everyone will see Him. (2) The Final Judgment will take place. Those who believed in Jesus will be declared innocent of sin; those who didn't believe in Him will be condemned to hell. (3) The resurrection of the dead will occur and believers in Jesus will receive new bodies designed to live forever. (4) The earth and universe as we know it will be cleansed of all evil and remodeled as the new heaven and new earth, free from all the disastrous effects of sin (see the Interlude). It will be the eternal home for all who believed in Jesus as their Savior. What would be a good way to describe the profound joy and peace of this existence in the new heaven and new earth? Read Isaiah 11:6-9 once more. There is the answer! By the way, this passage describes not only life in the new heaven and new earth but also life before the fall into sin.

What an honor for wolves and lambs, leopards and goats, calves and lions, cows and bears, and cobras and vipers! By describing them in a world in which all their hostile instincts have disappeared, Isaiah teaches us what life will be like in our eternal home.

Will There Be Animals in Heaven?

This passage from Isaiah also invites the question, "Will there be animals in heaven, in the new heaven and new earth?" Though the

Bible does not give a definitive answer, I believe the answer is yes! Since animals are not moral beings, they will not go to heaven on the same basis as humans, which is by faith in Jesus. Here is my logic:

If it is true that when God created this planet, He considered animals to be a vital component of His creation, and

If it is true that at the time of the Great Flood God took extreme care in assuring that the planet would continue to have animals on it, and

If it is true that through His suffering, death, and resurrection Jesus redeems humans and restores all aspects of His creation which were damaged by the fall into sin including plant life, animal life, and the physical planet itself (Matthew 19:28a, Acts 3:21 and Romans 8:21),

Then I believe that the new heaven and new earth will also be graced with the animals which God and we love so much. I don't think that specific pets will be there, like my boyhood cat Pregnant Pam or our beloved boxer Becky, but I do believe that all kinds of cats and dogs will be there. Wouldn't it be great to live on a planet where even wild animals are tame, loving and caring, which was their original purpose? Don't get me wrong; the main attraction of life in the new heaven and new earth will be getting to be with Jesus. But animals would only add to the beauty and joy of our eternal life!

In this chapter, we have only skimmed the surface of a great number of Bible texts in which the inspired authors refer to animals for the purpose of teaching important truths. Each of these texts demonstrates the love and admiration that God has for the animals He created. He truly is *The Greatest Animal Lover*!

CONCLUSION

I have attempted to show why humans have a special bond with animals. My thesis is that God loves and admires animals, and since we are created in His image, we do the same. To confirm this, it was necessary to provide evidence that God does indeed cherish animals more than anyone.

I have demonstrated six ways in which God shows Himself to be *The Greatest Animal Lover*. 1. He lovingly created animals with jaw-dropping design. 2. He attentively provides for them, both through the planet He created for them and in the command that humans should be their caretakers. 3. He faithfully rescued them at the time of the Great Flood. 4. In Bible times and today He applauds them by giving them special assignments in carrying out His will in this world. 5. He honors them in the Old Testament animal sacrificial system as they point to the future Messiah-Savior. 6. He values them by repeatedly referring to them while teaching important truths in His inspired Word, the Bible.

These six evidences of God's love for His animal kingdom are supported by abundant declarations throughout the Bible. One of my favorites is at the end of the Book of Jonah. God is disappointed at Jonah's lack of concern for the people of Nineveh who were spiritually and morally lost. In Jonah 4:11, as God expresses His sympathy for the inhabitants of the city, He doesn't forget the animals!

But Nineveh has more than a hundred and twenty thousand people who cannot tell their right hand from their left, and many cattle as well. Should I not be concerned about that great city?

It is clear that no one loves and admires animals like their Creator. Since He created us in His image, we also treasure animals. This truth does more than just answer an intriguing why question. It enables us to deepen our enjoyment of animals because we know that this relationship exists by God's design and for our good. As we grow in our appreciation of our special bond with animals we are led to thank and praise the God who created them and us!

ENDNOTES

1   https://www.americanpetproducts.org/press_releasedetail.asp?id=191
2   https://www.waza.org/about-waza/
3   https://www.chicagotribune.com/news/ct-gorilla-saves-boy-brookfield-zoo-anniversary-20160815-story.html
4   http://www.eurocbc.org/page158.html
5   https://www.worldatlas.com/articles/how-many-species-of-fish-are-there.html
6   https://www.nationalgeographic.com/science/phenomena/2013/10/22/of-70000-crustacean-species-heres-the-first-venomous-one/
7   https://en.wikipedia.org/wiki/List_of_marine_mammal_species
8   Radakov DV (1973) *Schooling in the ecology of fish.* Israel Program for Scientific Translation, translated by Mill H. Halsted Press, New York. ISBN 978-0-7065-1351-6
9   https://www.nationalgeographic.com/animals/mammals/b/blue-whale/
10 The World of Animals by Debbie and Richard Lawrence, 4th edition, 2016, Answers in Genesis, 2800 Bullittsburg Church Rd., Petersburg KY, 41080 (pages 24-27, 91-92, 97-111)
11 https://www.ck12.org/c/life-science/cartilaginous-fish/lesson/Cartilaginous-Fish-MS-LS/
12 https://oceanwide-expeditions.com/to-do/wildlife/sperm-whale
13 https://www.audubon.org/news/new-study-doubles-worlds-number-bird-species-redefining-species
14 Lawrence, pages 32-43, 82-89
15 https://www.mpg.de/7572084/bird-song-human-music

16 https://www.penguinworld.com/types/
17 https://www.worldatlas.com/articles/bat-species.html
18 Lawrence, pages 12-23, 28-30, 54-74, 82-90
19 https://animals.sandiegozoo.org/animals/marsupial
20 https://www.monkeyworlds.com/monkey-species/
21 https://www.worldatlas.com/articles/how-many-species-of-amphibians-are-there.html
22 https://www.worldatlas.com/articles/how-many-species-of-reptiles-are-there.html
23 https://www.iflscience.com/plants-and-animals/why-are-there-so-many-beetles-theyre-extinction-resistant/
24 https://www.space.com/41290-biggest-star.html
25 https://www.today.com/news/why-did-tiger-attack-roy-horn-2D80555372
26 https://abcnews.go.com/GMA/seaworld-trainer-dawn-brancheau-suffered-broken-jaw-fractured/story?id=10252808
27 https://www.greatfallstribune.com/story/news/local/2017/03/06/bike-collision-grizzly-determined-cause-fatal-encounter/98818710/
28 https://answersingenesis.org/
29 https://arkencounter.com/
30 https://answersingenesis.org/noahs-ark/how-could-all-animals-fit-ark/
31 Keil and Delitzsch, Commentary on the O.T., Vol. 3, p. 237, William B. Eerdmans Publishing Company, Grand Rapids, MI, reprinted, Sept. 1973.
32 https://answersingenesis.org/evidence-for-creation/god-created-plant-pollinator-partners/
33 https://biomimicry.org/biomimicry-examples/

SMALL GROUP BIBLE STUDY - CHAPTER 1A - 1D - CREATION

1. Do you have a favorite animal of the air, water, or land? What is it about this animal that catches your attention? Does anything about it remind you of its Creator?

2. In Chapter 1D the author gave some possible meanings (variety, beauty, and purpose) for the oft-repeated phrase, "It was good," in Genesis 1. Discuss other reasons why God saw that "it was good."

3. The New Testament emphasizes the role of God the Son (preincarnate Jesus) in the creation of all things. Read these passages: John 1:1-5; Colossians 1:15-17; and Hebrews 1:1-4.
    a. How does this information give us insight into the times Jesus frequently refers to animals (sheep, wolves, sparrows, foxes, snakes, doves, etc.) in His preaching and teaching?

    b. How do you imagine the three Persons of the Holy Trinity jointly participating in the creation of the animals? See Genesis 1:1, 26.

There are many creation statements throughout the Bible which include the creation of the animals on days five and six of Creation. Questions 4 through 9 take a look at some of these.

4. Read Nehemiah 9:5-6. In this first paragraph of a long prayer, God is praised for His created world.
   a. Which groups of created animals are included here?

   b. Think about "You give life to everything." How does this make you feel about our God?

5. Read Psalm 89:11. This is a psalm of praise to God.
   a. What do you believe is included in "all that is in it"?

   b. Ultimately, to whom do all animals belong? How does this affect how we treat them?

6. Read Psalm 104:24-25.
   a. In verse 24, what is implied by the words "in wisdom," "full," and "your"?

   b. Verse 25 reflects which specific verses from Genesis 1?

7. Read Psalm 148. It is an invitation to everything God has created, both inanimate and animate, to praise the One who made them. Now zero in on verses 7 and 10.
   a. Which groups of animals are invited to praise God? Why?

b.   How do they do this?

8.   Read Acts 14:8-19 (Paul evangelizing in Lystra) and Acts 17:22-28 (Paul evangelizing in Athens). Enjoy his creationist theology as part of his message to help his audience believe in Jesus. Now look more closely at 14:15 and 17:24-25.
     a.   What does Paul have to say about creation?

     b.   How does he use creation to invite people to believe in the true God?

9.   Read Revelation 4:9-11. For the moment, don't get bogged down in a study of "the living creatures" and "the twenty-four elders." Notice that God is praised not only for His salvation, but also for His creation.
     a.   How are the Creator and His creation described here?

     b.   The animals were created "by His will." It is only in Him that they "have their being." What does this say about God's relationship with the animals He created?

10. What insights have you gained through this study of the creation of the animals? Has it caused any change in your attitude about animals?

SMALL GROUP BIBLE STUDY,
CHAPTER 2 - PROVISION

1. A good place to begin studying the concept of God's provision for the animal world is with some words of Jesus. Read Matthew 10:26-31 and Luke 12:4-7. Reflect on Jesus' two declarations: "Not one of them will fall to the ground apart from the will of your Father," and "Not one of them is forgotten by God."

   a. What do these statements mean with respect to God's relationship with birds?

   b. Does this relationship extend to all animals?

   c. What do these verses say about God's omniscience?

   d. How do these ideas help us understand Jesus' statement in Matthew 6:26?

2. The author developed the idea that in the first four days of Creation God was preparing the planet not only for humans but also for animals.

   a. Briefly review together what God created on these four days and how each of these created elements was a blessing for animals.

   b. Of all these created elements which are perfect for animal life, which one captures your attention most? Why?

3. Psalm 104 is a celebration of how God provides for the animals through His created world.

   a. For each of the three sections below, explain (1) which element of God's creation is being highlighted and (2) in what ways it is a blessing to animals. Share what you like best about each section.

      i. Verses 10-13 –

      ii. Verses 14-18 –

      iii. Verses 19-22 –

   b. In verses 24-26, which group of animals is highlighted? Name some of your favorites from this group.

   c. In verses 27-30, how is God's relationship with the animals described? Do you think these verses mean that animals have a comprehension of God?

   d. In verse 29b do you see a connection to Jesus' words in Matthew 10:29?

4. Job 38-41 is a treasure trove of God's own remarks about the world He created. These comments come in the context of God in a way "talking smack" to Job, helping Job understand His sovereignty over the created world. Many of God's statements have to do with His beloved animals. As you read each section below, share what the

paragraph teaches us about God's relationship with, involvement with, and provision for the animals mentioned.

   a.   38:39-41 –

   b.   39:1-4 –

   c.   39:5-8 –

   d.   39:9-12 –

   e.   39:13-18 –

   f.   39:19-25 –

   g.   39:26-30 –

5. The author reviewed the Biblical mandate that we humans are to be caretakers of the animal kingdom. In other words, God cares and provides for animals through us. Read together Genesis 1:26-28 and Psalm 8:6-8. As a group, make a list of ways humans obey or disobey this mandate in our world today. Are you particularly passionate about any of these items?

6. Read Genesis 9:1-3. Here we see that God gives humans permission to kill and eat animals for our nutritional needs. How do we balance "kill and eat" with "take good care of them"?

7. From this study have you acquired new insights about God's provision for the animal kingdom?

SMALL GROUP BIBLE STUDY – INTERLUDE AND CHAPTER 3 – DAMAGED RELATIONSHIPS AND RESCUE

Interlude

The point of the Interlude is to explain why there is brokenness in the relationship between humans and animals.

1. Have you ever been stung by a bee or wasp, kicked by a horse, bitten by a dog, or scratched by a cat? Have mosquitoes ever ruined your picnic or termites your furniture? Share an experience with the group.

2. Adam and Eve's sin, and God's judgment on their sin, are the causes of all the disfunction and brokenness in our world. Genesis 3 describes how God's created world went from perfect to broken. Read the following sections of this chapter and discuss the implications for our world today.
    a. Verses 8-10 – Broken is man's relationship with God

    b. Verses 11-13 – Broken is the relationship between humans

    c. Verse 14 – Broken is the world of animals

    d. Verse 15 – Hope for renewal through the Messiah

e. Verses 16 and 19b – Broken is the human body

f. Verses 17-19a – Broken is the ground, the plant world and the planet itself

3. In Romans 5:15-17, how does St. Paul describe the brokenness caused by Adam's sin? How does he describe the hope mentioned in Genesis 3:15?

4. In Romans 8:18-23, St. Paul explains the cause of a broken world, the reality of this brokenness and the hope of total restoration. To expand on the comments of the author, read Paul's words and as a group explain the meaning of each verse.

5. In Chapter 6 we will talk more about how Jesus will undo the curse of brokenness and restore all to perfection on the Last Day. Enjoy together the hope provided by Acts 3:21, and Revelation 21:1-5.

Chapter 3

6. Unfortunately, many people believe the Great Flood and Noah's Ark are myths. The truth is they are historical realities which are important both for salvation history and understanding the fossil record.
   a. Read Matthew 24:36-39. What point does Jesus make about His Second Coming by referring to Noah and the flood? What do these verses teach us about Jesus' perspective of Noah and the flood?

b. Read Hebrews 11:7. What details do we learn about Noah in this verse? What is the point of view of the author of Hebrews about Noah, the ark, and the flood?

c. Read I Peter 3:18-22 and II Peter 2:4-10a. What is taught about Noah, the ark, and the flood in these two passages? What is Peter's stance on the account of Noah and the flood?

7. The author invites the reader to explore five components of the Great Flood. Skim the following sections of Chapter 3, and as a group ask questions, make comments, or point out ideas which are new and interesting.
   a. the man Noah

   b. the ark itself

   c. the floodwaters

   d. the animals (notice God's love for them)

   e. the God behind the flood

Special suggestion: Please try to organize a trip to the Ark Encounter for your family or Bible study group. You won't be disappointed!

SMALL GROUP BIBLE STUDY –
CHAPTER 4 – SPECIAL ASSIGNMENTS

In Bible Times

1. The author gave three examples of God giving animals special assignments in Bible times: Ravens Feed Elijah in I Kings 17:1-6; A Donkey Speaks God's Word in Numbers 22; and A Great Fish Redirects a Wayward Prophet in Jonah 1:17-2:10.

    a. Which of the three examples caught your attention most? Why?

    b. Did you learn anything new from these accounts about God's relationship with animals?

    c. Discuss any additional observations or questions about these three episodes.

2. Sometimes God used animals as instruments of punishment. Skim through the Ten Plagues in Exodus 7:14 - 11:10. God used animals in four of the ten plagues.

    a. Name the number of each plague and the animal used.

    b. What does this say about God's relationship with these animals?

3. Read II Kings 2:23-25. Once again, God used animals as instruments of punishment. These young men were from the town of Bethel,

famous for worshiping idols and rejecting God's Word preached by His prophets. The youth were mocking Elisha and telling him to go away.

    a. What might have been God's purposes in sending two bears to maul these young men?

    b. Discuss the possible reactions of the inhabitants of the town of Bethel.

    c. When people get mauled by bears today, is it this kind of direct punishment from God? Explain why or why not.

4. Read Luke 19:28-36. Here God uses an animal as a means of transportation.

    a. In your own words, how would you describe the assignment given to this young donkey?

    b. How was Jesus' relationship with this donkey different from our relationship with donkeys in general?

    c. Donkeys have a cross running across their shoulders and down their spines. Do you think Jesus noticed this during His Palm Sunday ride? What significance does this cross have for you?

Today

5. God assigns animals to provide for human needs. Do you value or love wool or silk for clothes, or eggs, milk or honey to eat? When we enjoy them, why might we be slow to thank God for the animal which provides them?

6. God assigns animals to entertain us. Share a recent experience in which you have been entertained by animals, either in a live setting or on the screen.

7. Read II Corinthians 1:3-5. God is a specialist at providing comfort to hurting humans. Do you think that in some cases He assigns animals to deliver His comfort? Can you give an example?

8. Read Psalm 103:1-5 and focus on verse 3b. Then read Luke 4:38-41 and focus on verse 40. Jesus is the Master Healer. Do you think that He assigns animals to deliver some of His healing? Can you give an example?

9. Review the section on biomimicry. If humans can improve their technology by studying animals, what does this say about animals? In what ways can we give their Designer Creator the credit for these new technologies?

SMALL GROUP BIBLE STUDY,
CHAPTER 5 – POINTING TO THE SAVIOR

1. The author mentioned four ways in which the sacrificial animals pointed to Jesus, the Savior of the world. For each point below, look up the passages and talk about the connection between the sacrificial animal and the Messiah Jesus.

    a. **It had to be perfect, without any defect.** – II Corinthians 5:21; Hebrews 4:15 and 7:26; I Peter 2:21-22; I John 3:5. Why did Jesus have to be sinless in order to save us? Is it difficult for us to grasp the concept of sinlessness? Why?

    b. **It became the owner's substitute in guilt and death.** – Which phrase(s) in each passage indicates "substitution"? Isaiah 53:4-6; Romans 4:25 and 5:6-8; I Corinthians 15:3; II Corinthians 5:21; I Peter 2:24 and 3:18; I John 2:2. Share how it makes you feel to think about Jesus being your Substitute in guilt and punishment.

    c. **It was sacrificed, and its blood was presented as evidence of death.** – Acts 20:28; Romans 5:9; Ephesians 1:7-8 and 2:13; Colossians 1:19-20; Hebrews 9:11-14; I John 1:7. These passages don't mean that Jesus' blood itself saves us. What is it that saves us?

    d. **It brought forgiveness of sins and atonement for the owner. It accomplished this not in and of itself, as Hebrews 10:4 says, but on the basis of Jesus' future sacrifice (Hebrews 10:5-14).**

e. Forgiveness – John 1:29; Acts 10:43 and 13:38; Ephesians 1:7; Colossians 1:13-14

f. Atonement – Romans 3:25a; Hebrews 2:17; I John 4:10
What is atonement between God and man? Why is forgiveness of sins necessary for atonement?

2. The author explained the process and meaning of the burnt offering by following the journey of an Old Testament family presenting their sacrifice. Imagine yourselves as part of this family. Read together the following verses and share your observations and how you might feel in each situation. Explain the Messianic meaning of each step.

a. Leviticus 1:1-3a – A member of your family chooses your animal. He is perfect in every way. You walk together to the tabernacle with your animal in tow. Depending on the economic situation of your family, your animal may be from the herd (v. 3), the flock (v. 10), or the bird cage (v. 14).

b. Leviticus 1:3b – As a family, you present your animal to the priest at the outer gate. Your perfect goat, sheep, bull, or bird is now your substitute.

c. Leviticus 1:4 – Your dad puts his hands on the head of your substitute and confesses the sins of the family.

d. Leviticus 1:5 – Your dad or the priests' helpers slaughter the animal. You watch as the priest takes some of the blood and sprinkles it on and around the Bronze Altar. The priest announces your forgiveness, as described in verse 4b, "on his behalf to make atonement for him." Your hearts are thankful for the renewal of God's forgiveness

e. Leviticus 1:6-9 – You watch as the priests prepare your dead animal to be completely burned. You ask the Lord to make you totally dedicated to Him.

3. Read Romans 12:1-2. How does our study of the burnt offering deepen our understanding of this passage?

4. We say that it is an honor to die for our country if for a just cause or to die for the sake of the spread of the gospel. Can we say that it was an honor for these animals to die for the cause of pointing Old Testament believers to their Messiah/Savior, Jesus Christ? Why or why not?

SMALL GROUP BIBLE STUDY, CHAPTER 6 – REFERRALS

1. Look up the following texts treated by the author and share any new insights or applications you learned or would like to add.
    a. Proverbs 6:6-8 – Ants and Hard Work

    b. Matthew 6:26 – Birds and Reducing Worry

    c. Matthew 10:29-31 – Birds and Reducing Fear

    d. Luke 13:34 – Hens and Jesus' Saving Ministry

    e. Matthew 7:15 – Wolves and False Prophets

    f. I Peter 5:8-9a – Lions and Satan

    g. John 10:11, 14a – Sheep and Believers in Jesus

    h. Malachi 4:2 – Leaping Calves and the Ultimate Joy of the Christian

i.   Isaiah 11:6-9 – Animals at Peace and Life in the New Heaven and New Earth

2.   The author presents an argument in favor of the possibility of animals forming part of the new heaven and new earth. What do you think? Why?

3.   In Matthew 10:16, Jesus prepares His disciples for their mission by referring to four animals! Explain what Jesus is teaching through His reference to each of the four. It may be helpful to have someone in the group google "10 Facts about" each animal. How does this teaching of Jesus apply to us as daily evangelists?

4.   In Luke 9:57-58, Jesus is teaching about the cost of discipleship. What specific lesson is Jesus teaching when He refers to foxes and birds? How does this apply to us?

5.   In Luke 13:31-33, Jesus calls King Herod a fox. What characteristics of a fox was Herod imitating? What is Jesus' point?

6.   God also honors eagles in the Bible. Have one person look up how many times eagles are mentioned, and another google "10 Facts about Eagles."
     a.   In Jeremiah 48:40 and 49:22, God's judgment on Moab and Edom is compared to a diving eagle. If you have time, read these whole chapters for the sake of context. In them, how is God's judgment like a swooping eagle?

b. Read Exodus 19:1-6, Psalm 103:1-5 and Isaiah 40:28-31. By referring to eagles in each text, what specifically is being taught about God's activity in our lives? Can you give an example in which God has worked in your life in one of these ways?

7. Aside from the texts mentioned in this study, do you have a favorite Bible passage which refers to an animal? What specific lesson is being taught in the passage?

8. The Holy Spirit often inspired His Bible authors to refer to animals in order to teach important truths. Do you agree that this is evidence that God loves and admires the animals He created? Why or why not?